PERILOUS TRAILS OF TEXAS

J. B. (RED) JOHN DUNN

EDITED BY

Murphy Givens & Jim Moloney
(Originally Edited by Lilith Lorraine)

PERILOUS TRAILS
OF TEXAS

J. B. (RED) JOHN DUNN

EDITED BY
Murphy Givens & Jim Moloney
(Originally Edited by Lilith Lorraine)

NUECES PRESS

Corpus Christi, Texas

Published by Nueces Press, 3435 Ocean Drive, Corpus Christi, Texas78411
www.nuecespress.com

Manufactured in the United States of America

First Edition

Library of Congress Cataloging-in Publication Number 2015902736

J. B. (Red) John Dunn: Perilous Trails of Texas / edited by Murphy Givens & Jim Moloney

Includes index.

ISBN   978-0-9832565-6-4

  1.   South Texas — History.
  2.   Nueces County — History.
  3.   Corpus Christi — History.
  4.   Texas Rangers — History.

Published by Nueces Press, Corpus Christi, Texas.

Cover design by Jeff Chilcoat

www.nuecespress.com

TABLE OF CONTENTS

PUBLISHER'S NOTE

Murphy Givens and I have now published seven books together. This book is a first for us as we have republished an existing book. "Perilous Trails of Texas" was printed in 1932. Today, copies are hard to find and very expensive, up to $750.

John B. (Red) Dunn's biography is an insight into the troubled times of the 1870s when South Texas was a wild and vicious land. Mexican raiders and Texan vigilantes fought battles that ended up punishing innocent settlers and ranchers.

This book is important to understand the long history of racial mistrust in SouthTexas. It gives a perspective into the raids and retribution which pervaded our area in the decades following the Civil War, when most of South Texas was scrub ranchland with a few small settlements and virtually no law enforcement.

Dunn uses words to describe black and Hispanic people which are no longer used in polite company or by thoughtful people. We have chosen to reprint his work as originally written because Dunn's writing conveys the attitudes prevalent among those living in this place and in that era.

Jim Moloney
Nueces Press
www.nuecespress.com

INTRODUCTION

John B. Dunn, born in Corpus Christi in 1851, wrote about his days as a Texas Ranger and vigilante rider in "Perilous Trails of Texas." In later, quieter years, Dunn displayed a collection of artifacts in his museum on Upriver Road.

Dunn's story gives us a perspective of the violent era of Reconstruction as told by one of the participants in many events. Dunn was involved in several bloody encounters between Anglo South Texans and Mexican-Americans in the rough times after the Civil War. It was a time when general lawlessness pervaded the land, darkening the days and threatening the nights.

Dunn was a Texas Ranger and hard-riding vigilante to whom every Hispanic was a Mexican and every black was, well, we won't use that word. If he was a racist, and he clearly was, convicted by his own words, then the men he rode with were likely of the same mind, mold and character. But whatever he was, Dunn has to be understood as a man of his time. And what a brutal time it was.

In Dunn's time, as told in "Perilous Trails," violence was ubiquitous. It was a time of undeclared warfare, a war of random encounter, with raids by bandits from across the border, with hide thieves roaming the cattle ranges and killing at will, followed by the punitive lynchings and extra-judicial killings by minutemen vigilantes who were quick with the rope and the gun and left a trail of dead.

In the wake of the most notorious outrages of the era, such as the robbery at Peñascal and the Nuecestown Raid, John Dunn was there, armed and in the saddle, pistols ready and rifle loaded and heart full of vengeance. Dunn's story must be read with a clear understanding of who he was and what the times were like. Perhaps he was not unusual, as a law-bringer and lawbreaker, as an avenging Ranger and a vigilante, and as a product of those violent times. We make no apology or defense. He was what he was. It is always difficult to judge the actions of the past since we cannot know first-hand the information or the experiences acted upon. But that doesn't mean we cannot or should not judge, otherwise there would be no progress in our understanding of what is right and wrong.

* * *

John B. Dunn's story begins with his father, Matthew Dunn, from Ireland, who came to Corpus Christi in 1845 with Zachary Taylor. The elder Dunn was a sutler, a storekeeper who sold supplies to the army. After the battles at Palo Alto and Resaca de la Palma, Matthew Dunn became a teamster so he could travel with the army into Mexico. He survived the massacre of an army supply train ambushed on the road to Saltillo. In the attack, wagons were burned and the teamsters and soldiers escorting the train were killed and their bodies mutilated. Only two men survived, Matthew Dunn and a man named Pritchett. Matthew later served as a courier and dispatch rider for Gen. Taylor until the end of the war.

After the war, Matthew Dunn returned to Corpus Christi and Henry Kinney gave him 100 acres on the old San Patricio Road five miles from town. Dunn married Sarah

Pritchett. She always believed that the man who escaped the wagon train massacre with Dunn was her long-lost brother, John Pritchett, but they were never able to locate him. Matthew and Sarah had three sons — John, born in 1851, Matthew, and James.

Matthew Dunn, the father, was a farmer and stockraiser. He was also a friend of Kinney. Young John, when he was a child, remembered Kinney visiting their place for Sunday afternoon cockfights.

In 1855, while working in the fields, Matthew Dunn suffered a sunstroke, which affected his mind. He was sent to New Orleans for treatment and apparently transferred to a hospital in Baton Rouge but all traces of him were lost. He was never found.

At the outbreak of the Civil War, the widow Sarah Dunn took her three sons to Gonzales to be near her relatives. Two of her sisters had married men in Gonzales.

At the end of the war, Sarah and her sons returned to the old Dunn homestead. In a yellow fever epidemic of 1867, John Dunn came down with the fever and sweated it out by sleeping between two sick cousins he was nursing.

When he recovered, Dunn went to Rockport to look for a job. He arrived at night and slept under a live oak. Next morning, he asked a man where the town was. "You're in the middle of it," he said. Dunn asked if the house at the end of the wharf was the only one in town. "No," the man replied, "there's another one." Dunn found a job hauling lumber then worked as a fireman on the old side-wheel steamer "Reindeer."

After a trip to St. Louis, Dunn returned to Corpus Christi, where he found three new beef packing houses operating on North Beach. "Instead of shipping cattle across the Gulf," Dunn wrote, "they built slaughter houses all over the country and commenced killing the cattle for their hides and tallow."

Dunn got a job in a packing house owned by Bill Brunwinkel and Henry Ball. His job, as a fireman, was to keep fire going in the steam boiler to heat the tanks where the meat was boiled for its tallow. The tallow, or fat, was poured into barrels and the hides were salted down to cure and fastened into bundles for shipment. Some of the meat was packed in salt and shipped as mess beef but most of it was dumped to rot outside the packeries.

John Dunn (known as "Red John" to distinguish him from a cousin also named John Dunn) left the packing house job and joined a company of Texas Rangers under the command of Bland Chamberlain.

There were 60 men in Chamberlain's company who were, Dunn wrote, the worst mixed lot of men who ever came together in one organization. One rode with guerrilla leader Charles Quantrill during the war and another, called Three-Fingered Jack, was wanted for murder in California. Chamberlain's company became notorious as the only company of Texas Rangers that ever mutinied in the field.

Chamberlain's and other Ranger companies were disbanded in 1870 when Gov. E. J. Davis established the State Police force to replace them. Dunn wrote that Chamberlain's Rangers were camped outside Austin, where they got drunk, then marched to the old Capitol to be discharged.

Dunn and other discharged Rangers were promised back pay and commissions in the new State Police force, Dunn said, but they never received the commissions or back pay. While waiting, Dunn worked for a time at King Ranch, cut hay for U.S. troops in San Antonio, and went up the trail with a cattle herd to Hays, Kansas.

When Dunn arrived back in Corpus Christi, he joined a vigilante group after George Hatch was killed at the north end of the Reef Road on Sept. 5, 1872. The murderers cut out the old man's pockets, robbed him, took his horses and fled.

Did the vigilantes catch up with the killers? Dunn explains in his memoirs. "Outside of five or six persons, no one knows whether they were caught or not." He said the names of the killers, made known to them, were written down for future reference. "It is amusing to hear people say that the murderers were never caught. Well, ignorance is bliss."

On May 9, 1874, a party of thieves killed four men at a store at the small community of Peñascal on Baffin Bay. In looking at the horse tracks near the store, a man in a posse noticed that brown sugar had leaked from one of the bags taken by the bandits, indicating the killers were heading not for the border, as the vigilantes had assumed, but for Corpus Christi.

John Dunn gathered his own posse of cousins and brothers to join in the search for the Peñascal killers. They found two suspects — Hypolita Tapia and Andres Davila — in a sheep pen, trying to blend in with the other sheep shearers who came up from Mexico. Dunn and the vigilantes took the two men to Meansville and placed them in a room under guard.

"We took Hypolita out and told him we wanted him to tell us all about the murders, but he would confess nothing," Dunn wrote. "We took him to a mesquite tree and let him kick a few chunks out of the horizon, after which he was ready to divulge everything."

Tapia and Davila were tried and hanged at Corpus Christi. After two of Tapia's brothers swore to get even,

Dunn began sleeping in his cornfield. One night, when he went back to the house to get a drink of water and, without thinking, lit a lantern, shots were fired at him from the darkness. After that close call, Dunn didn't want to risk another shot in the dark. He left to join the Texas Rangers.

Gov. Richard Coke disbanded the State Police created by E. J. Davis and re-commissioned special units of the Rangers in 1874. Warren W. Wallace was authorized to establish a company of Rangers as part of the newly created Frontier Battalion. Wallace's company made its headquarters at Concepcion, in Duval County. It was this company that Dunn joined.

Warren Wallace's company of Rangers got into trouble. These were truly killer Rangers. They were known as "rinches" (roaches) by Mexican-Americans and their activities helped give the Rangers a bad name in South Texas.

While Dunn was with Wallace's company of Rangers at Concepcion, the Rangers caught a man they called Moss Top for his head of unruly hair. They believed he had shot a fellow Ranger in the eye. The captain freed Moss Top but the Rangers later found him and lynched him in a brutal fashion. In Dunn's account, they took Moss Top into the brush, put his head in the fork of a mesquite and tied a rope to a saddle horn and broke his neck.

In another incident, at Lagarto, the lieutenant of the company, a man named Lark Ferguson, had a difficulty with the manager of a Mexican circus, who sprang at him and "Ferguson fired at him, striking him between the eyes. He put his foot on the Mexican's neck and fired two more shots into his head." Dunn was also accused in this slaying.

In Live Oak County, Dunn and another Ranger attacked the camp of two lonely shepherds (they were "Mexicans")

7

because they wanted their mutton that was roasting on the fire.

These and several other atrocities committed by Wallace's company caused some consternation in Austin. The company was disbanded in September 1874. The state's adjutant general, William Steele, said Wallace's company of Rangers had acted little better than a mob. Steele said in his criticism, "There is a considerable element in the country bordering on the Nueces that think the killing of a Mexican is no crime."

Dunn and several others were put on trial for robbery and murder. The trial was held at San Patricio but the trial records have been lost, consumed in a later courthouse fire. For once in his narrative, Dunn became terse and evasive. He was dismissive of the charges against him, saying he had been indicted for the disappearance "of every Mexican who did not respond when his mama called." Though we don't know the details of that trial, we know he was acquitted.

The emblematic raid of the era began when bandits rode in on Thursday, March 25, and camped on the Oso. On the next day, Good Friday, they stole horses and took men captive at two ranch houses. They killed an old man in the Juan Saenz community near Corpus Christi, captured travelers on the roads, and went on to Nuecestown. After some shooting and plundering at Noakes' store, the bandits took their captives and plunder and camped in the brush.

John Dunn was with a posse pursuing the bandits. His cousin, the other John Dunn, was in the same posse. As they approached the bandits' camp in the brush, shots were fired and the bandits decamped, leaving behind their hostages and plunder. A wounded bandit was captured and taken to Corpus Christi, where, without ceremony or legal prelude, he was hanged. All the other bandit raiders got away and slipped back across the Rio Grande.

Following the Nuecestown Raid, Dunn joined a band of militia riders headed by T. Hines Clark, a cattle rancher at Banquete. The militia chased thieves who killed cattle for their hides. At many of the ranches in the Big Sands, Dunn wrote, they found large buildings full of dried hides and pits dug in the sand filled with hides.

Sometime after a deaf sheep rancher named Thad Swift and his wife were murdered, a company of vigilantes rode up from Refugio, under the command of Henry Scott, the grizzled old vigilante leader. Dunn rode out to meet them. They asked him if he knew several people. Yes, he said, they lived on the Hill in Corpus Christi. Dunn rode with Scott's vigilantes into town, pointed out the men, and the posse captured them, tied their arms and legs, and rode away. The men they took were never seen again.

When Martha Rabb's son Lee was killed, the suspect was trailed by a posse of vigilantes to the border. Dunn wrote that "the know-it-alls say that he was never caught, but he was missing at all the elections since."

Dunn's "Perilous Trails in Texas" reveals the viral prejudice and vigilante violence in the rough times after the Civil War. The militia groups, the minutemen, and some of the South Texas Ranger companies were not known for restraint, nor for observance of legal formalities. In Dunn's point of view, the Rangers and vigilantes were making the country safe for Americans, meaning white people.

After a violent life in the saddle Dunn settled down to a quiet existence. He became a dairyman, married a woman named Lelia Nias, and opened a private museum at his place on Shell Road to display his collection of curiosities. Among other items, he had hundreds of guns from frontier times, including the pistol he took from Hypolita Tapia when he was captured in the sheep pen and there was a pistol that once belonged to Cortina.

John B. "Red" Dunn died on the last day of September 1940 when he was 89. The old Ranger and vigilante had ridden perilous trails in perilous times.

In his lifetime, Dunn belonged to a class of armed and angry men who cut a violent swath across South Texas. Dunn and the vigilantes he rode with inflicted whatever punishment they chose without the formalities of law. The death toll was never tallied, could not be tallied, but there were many left hanging on a lonely mesquite. Dunn justified this by saying, "I merely took St. Paul's advice and while in Rome did as the Romans." The raids and counter-raids, the lynchings and reprisal killings, left a lasting legacy of bitterness and ethnic enmity. The roots of that legacy can be found in Dunn's story.

Murphy Givens

ORIGINAL EDITOR'S FOREWORD

In presenting the memoirs of the oldest living pioneer of the Corpus Christi section I feel that the reader should be reminded that in practically every event narrated, the author was an actual participant. Without such a book as this much of the authentic history of Southwest Texas would be lost, or would be sadly distorted by younger authors, who, regardless of the honesty of their intentions, must depend for their material upon indirect information, upon what has been told them, rather than upon what has been carefully and conscientiously compiled from facts by those who were present when the scenes herein related were enacted.

Regarding the events described in these sketches, they have been related exactly as they occurred, told in the simple, direct style of the author, without any attempt to gloss them over, because the author has no apology to make. The reader, in order to understand many of the things that happened, must try to put himself in the place of the pioneers, in the place of the men who had the courage to go forth into an almost uncharted land and meet crude conditions with still cruder weapons.

If we, their descendants, living in the midst of the comfort and the safety that they have wrested from the untamed heart of nature and passed on to us to soften our lives and refine our sensibilities, have any word of condemnation to utter against them, the reflection falls not upon them but upon ourselves for our lack of understanding. Without them, we would not have been here, either to praise or to condemn. The very delicacy of sentiment that is ours is only the flowerage of civilization upon the topmost branch of the sturdy tree that they planted in the soil of the wilderness and watered with blood and tears. Ours is the fragrance of the flower, but theirs was the toil that rooted it deeply in the slime and nurtured it through the assaults of the inexorable elements.

It is in this spirit that the children of the pioneers and every reader of this book who reaps or squanders the heritage that they have given us should approach the threshold of those times when history was in the making.

Not in the spirit of judging their actions by artificial standards which in their day had no existence, but by asking ourselves if we in their places, should have acquitted ourselves as well, and by putting to ourselves the still more potent question: how well have we kept the birthright that they have given us, how well have we safeguarded the liberties that they purchased through untold privations, how courageously are we meeting the problems that confront us today; in short, when both we and they stand before the tribunal of a remote posterity, to whom shall the laurel be awarded, to the men who saw a wilderness and cleared it, who faced chaos and brought forth order; or to us, who, born in the midst of peace and plenty, now find ourselves floundering rather hopelessly in the quagmires of political impotency and spiritual confusion?

In presenting this book to the public, the author desires to pay tribute to the memory of the following men of outstanding character and of unfailing courage, without whose material support and moral encouragement, the rangers and those who took part in the events related in these memoirs would have been unable in many cases to accomplish what they did in making this section of the country safe for American civilization: T. Hines Clark, James F. Scott, Captain King, Martin Culver, Frank Biler, James Cody and William Cody. And to those men and to the rangers, early settlers and pioneers who cleared the dim and perilous trails of Texas that we may follow after in the light.

Lilith Lorraine *

* (Pen name of Dunn's daughter, Maude, Mrs. Cleveland Wright)

Red Dunn age 50

CHAPTER ONE

MY EARLY LIFE

My Birth And Earliest Memories — I was born on the 18th of January 1851 in the house that my father completed the same year; its construction was commenced in 1850. At that time there was but one home, belonging to a Mr. and Mrs. Finley,[1] between our place and the present town of Corpus Christi. This couple became my godfather and godmother. From our place to old San Patricio, a distance of 28 miles, there was not a single house.

It was customary in those days for people traveling back and forth to call at all the settlers' homes along the road and exchange news with one another. As we were the only settlers along the route, we enjoyed a monopoly of the news.

I remember several instances in which we were told by travelers that they had seen Indians while on their way down. Such yarns would give me the creeps at night.

One incident in particular made a deep impression on me. Some visitors said that as they were coming out of some timber close to Hart Lake[2] in San Patricio County they saw a bunch of about forty or fifty Indians over to their left.

---

[1] The 1850 census shows the name as J. Findlay and his wife Ann, with a large family.

[2] Hart Lake, or Hart's Lake, was an old watering hole for cattle and mustangs. It was located near the later town of Sharpsburg.

These Indians were coming out of the same timber and were going as fast as their horses could run. At first the travelers thought that the Indians were after them, so they concealed themselves in the brush and awaited developments.

But when the Indians reached the lake they rushed madly into the water, horses and all, and began drinking as though they were dying of thirst. Some of the horses could not get out and must have died in the lake. There was a drought and at that time the Nueces River became quite salty for several miles above.

There were several fights with Indians near Corpus Christi in those days. One was at the Rincon,[3] the land between the present port turning basin and the causeway, another was at Chocolate Motts on the Oso, and a third was at the San Jacinto Ranch.

Short Sketch of My Father's Life — My father was born in the county of Kildare, Ireland. Of his early life I have no knowledge. When General Taylor's army arrived in Corpus in September 1845, my father accompanied it as a sutler.[4]

In the spring of 1846 the army advanced to a point on the Rio Grande opposite the Mexican town of Matamoras. On the 8th day of May it met and defeated the Mexican Army at Palo Alto and again defeated the Mexican forces at Resaca de la Palma on the 9th. On the 18th day of May the American army crossed the Rio Grande into Mexico.

Before crossing the river, orders were issued that no civilians could accompany the army. As raw recruits were not being accepted, my father could not join the regular army but he was allowed to enlist as a teamster. All went

---

[3] North Beach.

[4] A sutler is a contract storekeeper for a military post.

well until the march on Saltillo. There the supply train that my father accompanied was attacked by a strong force of Mexican lancers. Most of the guards were killed or captured and all the drivers killed except my father and a man named Pritchett.[5]

After the massacre, my father acted as a courier and dispatch bearer until the war was over. After the war, he returned to Corpus Christi where he married my mother, whose name was Sarah Pritchett. She was a native of Missouri and always believed that the man Pritchett who escaped from the supply train massacre when my father did was a brother of hers, John Pritchett, from whom she had not heard for several years. My father never saw the man again and never learned whether he was captured or not.

Colonel Henry Kinney, the founder of Corpus Christi, and a friend of my father, made him a proposition. He told him that if he would build a house of specified dimensions, four or five miles west of Corpus Christi on the old San Patricio road, that he would give him a hundred acres of land. My father accepted the offer and built on the land, which is now owned by me, and which I have named Kinney Park in honor of Col. Kinney.

As I mentioned before, there was but one house between our place and Corpus Christi and from our house on to San Patricio, a distance of twenty-eight miles, there was not a single house.

When my father finished our house, he went to Gonzales and bought a few head of cattle from a man by the name of Zumolt. This man's brand was a single "Z". We adopted

---

[5] Mexican guerrilla forces captured the supply train on Feb. 24, 1847. They destroyed more than 150 wagons filled with army supplies and slaughtered the captured teamsters by the most horrible means. From "Mexican War Journal" by Capt. Frank Smith.

this as our brand and always used it. My father also engaged in farming.

My Mother's Life — My mother was born in Greene County, Missouri. She had four sisters: Caroline, Martha, Eliza and Francis, and two brothers, John and David. David, the elder brother, settled in DeKalb, Red River County, Texas, and was postmaster there for a number of years. His sister Caroline made her home with him and his family until her death. My uncle John I have mentioned before as having been believed by mother to be the other man who escaped from the supply train when my father escaped.

My mother's other sisters settled in Gonzales County, Texas. My Aunt Martha married James Hodge of that county. Francis married W. S. Lowry of the same county. After her death Mr. Lowry married her sister Eliza. Many members of these families are still living in the same locality.

When I was about four and a half years old, my father suffered a sunstroke which deranged his mind. As there was no asylum in this state at that time, he was sent to New Orleans, La. From there they claim that he was transferred elsewhere, but we were never able to locate him.

After he was sent away, my mother remained on the old homestead and did the best she could for us. She had three children: Matt, James, and myself. I was the eldest and James was the youngest.

When the Civil War began, our two uncles, Hodge and Lowry, came to Corpus Christi and moved us, our cattle, and everything to Gonzales.

We had some amusing experiences after reaching there. To enable the reader to appreciate them I explain that we had been raised in an Irish settlement where the Irish brogue was spoken. Never having heard anything else, we spoke it fluently. Therefore, we caused as much excitement in our new locality as a circus, especially among the "swamp angels" from the Guadalupe bottoms and the "hillbillies" from the post oaks across the San Marcos River.

They would come for miles on Sundays to hear us "chirp," as they called it. Having arrived at the scene of the entertainment, one of them would say, "Stir them up, make them say 'sumpfin',"" and when we responded they would throw back their heads and let out yells that would cause a Comanche Indian to turn green with envy. This is not intended as a reflection upon the people of that section in general, for some of the best people I have ever known lived there. If the "swamp angels" and "hillbillies" that I have mentioned had come to Corpus Christi, they would have caused as much excitement among the "shanty Irish" as we caused among them. It would have been on the same principle as the predicament of the fellow who was exhibiting a white moose.

This showman had a sign pinned to the front of his tent which read, "whole families admitted for one dollar." The first one to come in was an old farmer who had a large crowd following behind him. He paid his dollar and walked right into the tent while the ticket seller was counting the crowd. When he came to number twenty-two, he sent an employee in to catch up with the old man and bring him back. The showman questioned him, saying, "Is all this your tribe?" "Yes, sir," replied the farmer. "Then go ahead," said the showman, "it will be as big a treat for my moose to see them as it will be for them to see the moose."

The Treatment of Father Padee — Another incident worthy of mention happened at Gonzales a short time before we

19

arrived there. It will give the reader an idea of how people act who are blinded by prejudice.

There was a Catholic priest at Hallettsville whose name was Father Padee. He was the priest who baptized me and I knew him very well. Once while on his way to San Antonio, he was delayed and had to stop overnight at Gonzales. The rumor was spread that there was a priest at the hotel, so a mob gathered which went and took him from his room. The mob forced two negroes to put a rail on their shoulders on which they rode the unfortunate priest all over town, abusing and insulting him in every possible manner.

The "Lady" with the Hood — It was customary during war days in Gonzales for the people to crowd around the stage stand, called in those days the Keyser House. There one could get the first news.

One day there were several passengers on the stage. Among them was a small-sized woman well-dressed. She wore a small head-dress called a hood. When she got off the stage, instead of going down the sidewalk, she started across the plaza. An old rube was leaning against one of the posts watching her. He started to say something but had first to get rid of a quarter of a plug of tobacco that he had in his mouth. This operation completed, he remarked, "If that is not a man, you all can eat my hat."

One word brought on another until at last two or three agreed with him and accompanied him to halt the alleged "lady." They took "her" to the guardhouse where some soldiers were stationed and sure enough "she" proved to be a man. The man told his captors that he was General McGruder's[6] ambulance driver on Galveston Island and

---

[6] He was no doubt referring to Gen. John B. Magruder, who was among prominent Confederates who fled to Mexico at war's end.

that he was trying to get to Mexico. He was put in jail and that was the last I ever heard of him.

Thieves on Padre Island — In the year 1862, ships of the federal fleet were stationed at the old Corpus Christi Pass, which at that time was navigable only by small boats. The federals were dependent for their meat supply upon a bunch of Mexican renegades and white traitors. These thieves would rob the people of their cattle and deliver the meat to the fleet.

Captain Ware[7] of the Confederate Army, who commanded a company here, took ten men and went to Padre Island to capture the thieves. When he came in sight of them, he found them strongly entrenched in the sandhills and saw that they had about 40 men. He called for a volunteer to go under a flag of truce to ask them to surrender.

Lawrence Dunn Volunteers — Lawrence Dunn, who could speak the Mexican language well, volunteered to go. He tied a white handkerchief to the top of his gun barrel and rode over. He talked to them a few minutes then turned his horse to ride back.

Murdered Under a Flag of Truce — Someone in the bunch fired a shot. With that, his horse began running and they saw him hanging on one side. His brother Matt and a few others rode out to meet him and helped him from his horse. He spoke only one sentence, "had bad luck," and died.

At the time of Lawrence Dunn's murder, he was suffering from a broken arm caused by a (rifle) ball which

---

[7] Capt. James A. Ware commanded troops in the Corpus Christi-San Patricio area in Col. Rip Ford's Cavalry of the West.

he received during the bombardment of Corpus Christi by the federal fleet a short time previous.

The Suspect and His Motive — White traitors who were in the bunch said that a Mexican named Tom Basquez fired the shot. It seemed that Nicholas Dunn, a brother of Lawrence Dunn, found this man driving a number of horses to town and in order to recover one of his own that had strayed in among them, he reprimanded the Mexican, threatening to have him arrested if he ever drove his horses out of the range. For this the Mexican had a grudge against Nicholas and those of his name.

Basquez Is Honored — After the war, Basquez was looked on as a patriot and was put on the Corpus Christi police force. He is the same man whom the Peñascal murderers claimed to have originated the murder and robbery there, but although they swore to this testimony I do not think the unpleasant subject was ever broached again.

CHAPTER TWO

AFTER THE CIVIL WAR

A Clash with Wesley Hardin — John Wesley Hardin, the noted desperado, was living in Gonzales County when E. J. Davis, Reconstruction governor of Texas, appointed a number of negro police. Among them was a blacksmith named John Lackey and another man named Green Parmore.[8] Both lived in Gonzales County.

One day[9] they were sent out on Sandies Creek to arrest a white man. There was a small country store at the place called "Dan Foe's." When they went into the store, Hardin was sitting in a chair.[10] On seeing them, he asked, "Who the devil are you two?" Lackey spoke up, saying, "We are policemen, we are!" Hardin said, "The hell you are!" and jerked out his pistol, killing Parmore the first shot. Thereupon Lackey jumped through the window, but before he could make good his escape, Hardin shot him through the jaw, cutting his tongue in two. But he got away and hid in a pond of water where he was found and taken to Gonzales. There he recovered and lived for years afterward.

---

[8] His name was Green Paramore. From "The Sutton Taylor Feud" by Chuck Parsons.

[9] The date was Oct. 19, 1871.

[10] The store was owned by Neill Bowen, Hardin's future father-in-law. Hardin was eating cheese and crackers when Green Paramore approached him. From "John Wesley Hardin" by Leon Metz.

After the killing of Parmore, the rest of the negroes went wild. The incident happened on Friday and on Saturday the negroes congregated around Lackey's blacksmith shop swearing vengeance. They were armed with all kinds of old rusty rifles that looked as if it would be impossible to knock the hammers down with a hammer.

The mayor at that time was a German named Keyser. He sent some men to watch the hardware stores and took three men armed with shotguns over to the shop where the negroes were congregated. He pulled out his watch and held it up to them, saying, "You black devils have just fifteen minutes to get out of town." They milled around for a moment or so and an old negro on a mule started off in a trot that soon became a gallop and before the fifteen minutes were up all had disappeared.[11]

We Return Home — After the war, we moved back to the old home in Corpus Christi. The town was a desolate looking place. It had suffered bombardment during the war and was badly shattered. There were several companies of negro soldiers stationed there and the citizens were subjected to all kinds of humiliation and insults from them. It was a common occurrence for them to walk into private homes and demand coffee or food.

My Uncle Has Visitors — One Sunday two of these negro soldiers went to the home of one of my uncles, John Dunn,

---

[11] A more detailed account was in the San Antonio Herald, Oct. 31, 1871, which said the freedmen assembled in numbers with plans to go after Paramore's killers when the sheriff and mayor intervened. "Every effort is being made by the good people of the county to bring the murderers to justice. The two freedmen were members of the State Police." Much hostility existed against the black members of the State Police.

living four miles west of town. They entered the house while the family was away at church and dressed themselves in some of the boys' clothing. They armed themselves with some of the pistols from the place and left.

When the family returned from church and found the strange guns and uniforms, they knew who had done the work. One of the boys, Matt Dunn, went to army headquarters and reported the matter to the officer in charge. The officer was quite insulting and denied flatly that it was any of his men.

But next morning Matt got there before roll call and saw that two names were not answered. He called the officer's attention to the matter, but the officer flew into a tantrum and still tried to deny that any of his men had taken part in the robbery. He told Matt that if he was so sure about the matter to go and get the deserters and not to bother him about it.

The Deserters Are Captured — Matt went in the direction of the present causeway, [12] thinking the negroes might have crossed the reef[13] which was there at that time. When he got to the reef he found a fisherman who told him that he had seen the negroes about two hours before and that they had gone out on a peninsula that ran into the Nueces Bay and that he had not seen them since.

Matt went out on the peninsula and found them near its point. When they saw him coming they pulled out their pistols and told him to stay back. He ordered them to surrender. They began shooting at him.

Matt opened fire on them and when all his leads were gone but one, he charged them and killed one of them. At

---

[12] The Nueces Bay Causeway.

[13] The oyster shell reef dividing Corpus Christi Bay and Nueces Bay was used as an underwater road or bridge.

that the other one ran into the bay and got bogged in the mud. Matt roped him and dragged him to shore. He tied his hands behind him and put the rope around his neck, driving him ahead of him through town and into the barracks where he turned him over to the commanding officer. This personage thereupon changed his tune. He was now all pie and politeness and could not think of enough apologies.

More Visitors — About a month after that a corporal and four negro privates came to our house. There was no one at home but myself and my two brothers. The intruders entered with bayonets on their guns and asked us where the rest of the family was. We told them there was no one at home but ourselves. They asked our names and we told them it was Dunn. They said they wanted to see a man by that name *bad*. We offered to send one of the boys for him, but one of the negroes said, "I guess not!"

They ordered us to "hustle around" and get them something to eat. We began getting in wood to make a fire and during these operations I whispered to my brother Matt and told him to jump on a horse and go after my cousin Matt (the same one who had gone after the deserters and killed one of them).

My brother had been gone only a few minutes when one of the negroes asked, "Where is the other boy who was here?" "I guess he got scared," I answered, "and ran off to the brush."

With that this negro winked at his companions and they all went outside into the chaparral. About fifteen minutes after they left, the two Matts rushed up on horseback armed with shotguns and pistols. They searched the brush about an hour but found no trace of the negroes and never heard of them afterwards. This Matt Dunn was the same man who was murdered at Petronila (see later sketch) and a brother of Lawrence Dunn who was murdered on Padre Island.

Yellow Fever — In the month of July 1867, a small vessel came into Corpus Christi from Tuxpan, Mexico loaded with bananas. The Mexicans on the boat loaded a dray with some of the fruit and sent the dray man to peddle it around. Almost everyone who ate the fruit took the yellow fever.[14]

The first one to die was a blacksmith by the name of Drinkard. He died that night shortly after eating the bananas.

At this time I was working in a hay camp down on the Oso Creek with Matt Dunn, (the same man mentioned in the previous sketch) and his two brothers, Pat and Joe. There was also a Belgian there named August Vandavell, who had been a member of Maximilian's army in Mexico and who had fled with other ex-soldiers when Maximilian was captured.

The evening after the banana boat came in, word came to camp that Christie Dunn,[15] a brother of the boys with whom I was working, had lost his wife and that he was dying.

On hearing this we broke camp and went to town. Christie lived on the first corner south from the present location of the First State Bank. When we reached Corpus, we stopped our wagons across the street from Christie's house in front of a store that had living rooms above it. The boys got out of the wagon and went into Christie's house.

The man who owned the store was named Poland. We heard a noise on the porch upstairs and, looking up, saw

---

[14] Most accounts attribute the outbreak of yellow fever to a visitor named J. S. Snyder who was already sick when he came to Corpus Christi from Indianola, where the fever raged.

[15] Christopher Dunn.

Poland come staggering out. He let out one of the most blood-curdling yells I have ever heard and screamed, "Molly is dead!"[16] Molly was his wife. For months afterward I could hear that scream in my sleep.

A few minutes later some of the boys came out of Christie's house and told us that Christie's wife was dead and that they thought Christie was dying. By that time the fever was all over town.

We returned to the ranch which was about four miles from town. That evening the Belgian, August, and I came back and dug the grave for Christie's wife and next morning we had to open it to put Christie's coffin on top of hers. By this time more of the family came down with the fever.

The next day Joe Dunn died, and two days later his mother followed him. The following day Pat Dunn passed away. Four members of the family recovered. August, the Belgian, was the last of our dead, a considerable number, if one takes into account the total population at that time.

A Large Family — There were eight members of the particular Dunn family mentioned in this article. Their names were Christie, Nicholas, Pat, Matt, Lawrence, Mike, Joe and John. John was the youngest and is the only member of the family living at the present writing. Lawrence Dunn (see previous sketch) was murdered under a flag of truce during the Civil War and Matt Dunn (see later sketch) was murdered by Mexican bandits at his ranch on Petronila Creek. Pat and Joe died of the yellow fever and Mike and Nicholas died of other ailments.

---

[16] Mrs. John Pollan. From the *Corpus Christi Advertiser*, Aug. 14, 1867.

A Discharged Soldier Finds a Refuge — In 1865 and on the spot where the Nixon building now stands, there was a two-story building with dormer windows facing the bay. This building belonging to the Meuly family was vacant.[17] It had a large cellar underneath.

One day a discharged soldier came from Brownsville, broke and unable to engage board. So he went upstairs in this old building and slept there at night. In the daytime, he did odd jobs on the wharf, helping to unload boats, etc. The first week he hardly made enough to buy food, according to what he told some of the boys who used to prowl around the building.

Another Refugee — On Monday of the soldier's second week at the old house, an old Mexican came up and took charge of the cellar under the building. That week the white man did very well, as there was a steamer in and several schooners. When he received his pay it amounted to five dollars.

The Soldier Is Murdered — The old Mexican had been down on the wharf all evening and must have seen the soldier receive his pay. That night he murdered the soldier.

He was the first murdered man I had seen. We discovered the body in the following manner:

We Hunt A Good View — A steamer was due that morning and we wanted to see it coming in. As the Meuly building on the bluff was higher than most others and commanded a better view of the bay, we ran upstairs to get a good view of

---

[17] The Meuly house on the bluff, which was vandalized by occupation troops after the war, was torn down in October 1871. From the Nueces Valley, Oct. 21, 1871.

the incoming boat. We were right on the murdered man before we realized it.

A Horrible Discovery — He had been stabbed to death in a brutal manner. His throat was cut and he had been run through the breast several times. His arms and wrists were slashed from trying to ward off the knife. One stab in the breast went through to the floor and blood still dripped from it. The murderer must have taken the knife in both hands and thrown his whole weight on it, working it backwards and forwards. In a few moments, the news was all over town and the murderer was being sought. But he had disappeared.

Capture of the Criminal — That night he was captured about a mile from town. He was found standing on a box outside a window, trying to raise it and get inside. He was confined in jail for over a year but while there he took dysentery and died before his trial came up.

He Becomes A Songwriter — While in jail, he composed a song about Charley, the man he murdered, and he would sing it every day. He had been educated for a priest and would go through the whole Mass every Sunday. He even acted as his own organist, using his window sill as the keyboard of his organ. All the time he was going through the ritual he would vary it by throwing the contents of his slop bucket upon people outside who came within his range. After he had done this he would continue with the Mass as though nothing had happened. I have his knife in my museum.

CHAPTER THREE

MY ADVENTURES BEGIN

Experiences at Rockport — After the yellow fever epidemic, I went to Rockport and worked with the Powell family who lived four miles from that place. At that time there were only two houses in Rockport, one belonging to an old turtle fisherman named Andy Johnson, and the other, near the foot of the wharf, belonging to a man named Mathis.[18] I arrived there on horseback late at night and camped under a live oak tree near the foot of the wharf.

A little before sunrise a couple of men came strolling down to the wharf. I went out and met them and asked them where the town of Rockport was. They looked dumbfounded and one of them finally answered, "You are right in the middle of the town now, sir." I asked if the house near the wharf was the only one in town and he said, "No, sir, there is the other one," and pointed to a small cabin a short distance away under some live oaks. I inquired if there were any stores and he said, "Yes, the old man out on the head of the wharf who attends to the

---

[18] Thomas Henry Mathis (for whom the town of Mathis was named) and his cousin John M. Mathis owned a wharf and warehouse at Rockport shortly after the war. From "Aransas" by William Allen and Sue Hastings Taylor.

warehouse keeps a few things." I went out and invested my last quarter in crackers and sardines.

Just as I had finished my banquet I saw a wagon drawn by a yoke of oxen. Two men were in the wagon. I followed them down on the wharf and asked one of them for work. He told me that he was hauling lumber from the steamer to the lumber yard and that they were starting at once and if I would work for fifty cents a day I could begin. I accepted the offer.

The man who had the hauling contract was named Billy Powell and the man who was driving the wagon was Frank Bogus.[19] This latter person I shall have occasion to mention in describing our intended invasion of Guerrero, Mexico. He was a giant in strength. I have seen him strike an ox with his fist and make the animal bellow with pain.

Bogus Gets into an Argument — Bogus once had some trouble with another man at Borden's Ferry on the Nueces River. Bogus was on the north bank of the river and the other man on the south bank when they began abusing each other. At last the man called Bogus a pet name. With that, Bogus jumped into the ferryboat and began pulling to the other side, whereupon the other fellow opened his pocket knife and stuck the blade into a tree to make a rest for his pistol. He knelt and took deliberate aim at Bogus as he pulled the boat across. When he fired the last shot, he broke and ran, throwing his pistol away as he went. When Bogus got ashore he chased the fellow about a mile up the river where he ran into a house and hid under a bed, begging the lady of the house to protect him. This she did by inducing Bogus to go away.

---

[19] His name was Frank Boggus.

I Get A Firing Job — After I had finished with the hauling job, I worked with Billy Powell's father until sometime in '68. They were fine people. In the meantime, Rockport went through a big boom as the steamers were coming in every week and taking cattle to New Orleans. The first two steamers belonged to independent parties. They were named "The Dudley Buck," a propeller, and the "Reindeer," an old sidewheeler. I fired on both of them for several trips until they were both wrecked.[20] It was claimed that Morgan got one of his pilots aboard these steamers to do the work and then employed him to pilot his own steamer. Let me say right here that firing on these tubs was no picnic.

I Meet Jim Brennan — One day I happened to go down to the wharf when there was a steamer in, and whom should I see aboard but a fellow by the name of Jim Brennan, who worked at my uncle's at the time of the yellow fever epidemic and whom I had helped to nurse through his attack. He was a middle-aged man and I thought a lot of him. When he informed me that he was going back to New Orleans on the boat and from there to Milwaukee, I was anxious to go with him. He asked me how I was fixed for money and I told him I had about $140 and a horse, saddle and pistol.

He said, "It's foolishness for a young man to waste all his life in Texas when up in Milwaukee he can make more in a month than he could earn here in six months." After a little persuasion, I agreed to go with him.

---

[20] The "Reindeer" wrecked on the bar at the Aransas Pass in February 1870. From "Padre Island" by Writers' Round Table.

I Leave Rockport for Milwaukee in 1868 – After agreeing to go with Brennan to his home in Milwaukee, I returned to Powell's and collected what was due me. I sold my horse, saddle, bridle and pistol, which raised my cash account to one hundred and sixty dollars. When I got back to the boat Brennan told me that they were short a fireman and that if I would fire during the trip, I could get my passage free. I was glad to do this.

We Reach St. Louis — When we got to New Orleans, we took passage aboard the "Pauline Carrol" for St. Louis. There was a crowd of tough-looking men aboard the ship and I noticed that they kept close together. We had our baggage piled up and one of us always stayed and watched it. One day while our crowd was walking around and I was on guard, one of the other crowd said to me, "What are you watching?" I replied, "I am watching these valises." He said, "If I catch you watching them again, I will break your nose." With that he jumped and struck me on the nose.

He was a very small young fellow and I hardly felt the blow, but after that the whole crowd jumped on me. There happened to be the wreckage piled up near us and when I saw my plight, I jerked up a long bolt of iron and kept them at bay until our crowd came up. They had gotten within a few feet of each other when the other crowd all sat down on their luggage and one of our men caught me and pulled me back.

The Mystery Explained — I could not understand what was the matter until the man who had pulled me back explained that they were all Odd Fellows[21] and could not fight each

---

[21] Independent Order of Odd Fellows, a fraternal and benevolent lodge.

other. However, the man who got struck with my iron rod was not an Odd Fellow and could not be pacified, so they let him fight with a gambler in our crowd who soon cooled him down.

Brennan Has An Accident — A few nights after the fight, Brennan lost his hat. It probably blew overboard or some deckhand picked it up. He began searching the whole ship and happened to get too near the Pitman beam, which struck him on the side of the face, splitting it from his forehead down to the side of his neck. He was a large red-complexioned man and already had a wound on his chin made by what was called a "buck and ball" during the Civil War. One buckshot was still in his chin. This wound, together with his later accident, did nothing to contribute to his beauty.

My Confidence Is Betrayed — I had all the confidence in the world in Brennan. I had nursed him through the yellow fever and on this trip I had turned my money over to him to keep for me. We used to lie on blankets on deck at night with our valises under our heads. As we had to stop quite often along the route and were not expecting to get to St. Louis until morning, I had placed my valise under Brennan's arm and walked aft as the boat was landing. On returning to where I had left Brennan, I found he was gone with both my money and the valises. The watchman said that he was the first man ashore.

That was the last I ever saw or heard of him, but there I was, nearly two thousand miles from home with not a penny in my pocket, and the only clothes I had were on my back. I could not make myself believe that Brennan would treat me this way. With his face disfigured as it was, the police could have caught him in a few hours.

I Hobnob with Hoboes — The next evening, I followed a railroad track out into the suburbs and just about midnight crawled into a coal car that was on a siding. A little later a crowd of hoboes came into the car and began hitting me with pieces of coal. Feeling that my presence was slightly unwelcome, I emigrated to a small garden where there were a couple of stacks of hay. There I fared better than in the coal car. The next morning, I beat it back to St. Louis, following the river, until I came to a place where some wagons were unloading a lot of burned stuff from a store that had been destroyed by fire the night before.

There were a lot of hoodlums scratching around in the ashes and I noticed that some of them were finding pocket-knives that were scarcely scorched at all. I fell in line and soon had both pockets filled with fairly good knives. The last one I found was a beauty. Just as I picked it up, a large boy who was in the gang walked up and asked me if I would sell it, and how much I wanted for it. I told him that I would sell it for a quarter, which he willingly gave me.

I told him that I was hungry and wanted to buy something to eat. He invited me to come with him, saying that his brother was a foreman in the St. Louis type foundry, and inviting me to eat dinner with them. I was glad to accept this invitation and made arrangements with the old German lady who kept the boarding house for a few days' board until I could find a job.

I Return Home — Three days afterward, I crossed over to the Illinois side and obtained work on a farm. I remained there until October, being sick practically all the time. At last I returned to St. Louis and boarded the steamer "Stonewall" for New Orleans. From New Orleans I went to Galveston and from there to old Indianola where I took the mailboat for Corpus Christi.

About the first news that I heard from Corpus when I landed in Galveston was that Matt Dunn had been murdered by Mexican robbers.

Murder of Matt Dunn — Matt and Pat Dunn, previously mentioned as brothers of John and Mike Dunn, owned the Petronila Ranch west of Corpus Christi. The ranch was well-stocked with cattle, horses, and sheep. In 1867 Pat died with the yellow fever and Matt stayed alone on the ranch with his men. His foreman was a man named Juan Franco.

One day some strange Mexicans came and camped on the creek a little way from the main crossing. They went to the house and asked Matt for things such as salt, rice and meat. He gave them all they asked for. The next morning, they came for more supplies, which he also gave them. Afterwards he went off on a horse hunt and did not return until late in the evening.

When he arrived at the ranch he found the Mexicans there. As he was unsaddling his horse, one of them put a pistol to the back of his head and the other one between his shoulders and both fired, killing him instantly. They robbed the place, taking everything of value, including the best horses on the ranch and fled to Mexico.

A Different Story — This was the story told by the head man, Juan Franco. We knew no better until we captured Hypolita Tapia (see later sketch) and he gave us a list of the names of the men who were in the plot, naming Juan Franco as the originator.

Tapia said that as Matt had a mail route, Corpus to Brownsville, Juan knew it was payday and supposed that Matt's money had come in the mail.

As soon as Franco heard that Tapia had given him away, he lost no time getting to Mexico.

CHAPTER FOUR

I WORK IN SLAUGHTERHOUSES

Changes at Home — When I got back to Corpus, it seemed that everything had undergone a complete change. Instead of shipping cattle across the Gulf, they built slaughterhouses all over the country and commenced killing the cattle for their hides and tallow. The process they used was something like this:

A certain number of cattle would be driven out of a large pen into a small chute. A man with a long spear would get on a plank or walk above the cattle and stab them in the back of the neck. This would sever the spinal column and they would drop dead. They were hauled on to the skinning floor by a block and tackle pulled by a horse. There the butchers skinned them. The gut man, as he was called, cut the carcass open and took out the entrails. In the meantime, the hide man had taken the hide to a vat where it was salted down. Then the marker cut the hams and shoulders, marking them where the bones were to be broken and marking where the ribs joined the back bone. After this, the ax man broke all the bones where they were marked. The meat was dragged outside and pitched on platforms near the tanks until there was enough to fill the tanks into which it was transferred. The steam was turned on and the meat was cooked so thoroughly that you could take the large joint bones in your hands and mash them to powder.

Sometimes they would run out of cattle and the meat would lie on the platforms two or three days in the hot weather and by the time we secured more cattle it would be so rotten and full of maggots that the stench was suffocating.

I did all kinds of work at this time, but mostly firing and cooking. When I first started working in the slaughterhouse it was in what was called the Rincon, the strip of land between the present turning basin and the causeway.[22] There were three slaughterhouses at that time in this section of the country. One belonged to old man Deavilin,[23] one to John Hall, and the third to two men named Bill Brunwinkel and his partner, Mr. Ball. They were known as Bill and Ball. Bill afterward bought out Ball's interest and ran the business alone.

I Get Up Steam — The first work I obtained was as a fireman, in Bill's employ. The engineer's name was Fee and he was known as Captain Fee. He hired me in the evening and told me to get up early the next morning and get up steam and that by the time that was done he would be there. I was so pleased to get my job that I arose before daylight and started a fire in the furnace.

I had seen other firemen throw the shin-bones of slaughtered cattle into the furnace to raise steam quickly, as the bones were full of oil and would make a very hot fire. I followed their example and in a short time everything was sizzling from the heat.

The steam gauge was on top of the boiler and when I happened to look at it, I saw that it had about all the steam it would carry. I hardly knew what to do until I spied a long pole leaning against the boiler. I had noticed the engineer

---

[22] What is now called North Beach.

[23] Alonzo A. DeAvalon, a Frenchman who came to Corpus Christi in 1859, operated a beef packing house on North Beach.

using it to raise the handle or beam of the whistle to cause it to blow. So I took the pole and gave a few blasts.

I looked towards the house where the engineer was sleeping and saw him coming in his nightgown. He made a comical figure in this garb with his long black beard. Just as soon as possible, he let the steam off and turned to me and said, "Young man, in a few more minutes you would have been sailing through space."

Crawford Plans Dark Deeds — After staying in the Rincon a few months, Bill moved the slaughterhouse down to the mouth of the Oso Creek. As he could get no cook, he raised my wages on condition that I would change jobs and do the cooking. He hired a new engineer named Crawford to run the engine. Crawford used to give me fifty cents to stay up and fire and watch the engine at night for a few hours. When Bill found out I could be trusted with the engine, he made up his mind that he would cut expenses by discharging Crawford and by making me tend to the engine half the night besides cooking for the men. So he began to get cross with Crawford and eventually discharged him.

Crawford came and told me what Bill had done and said to me, "Just watch me. I'll move him up to the moon for this." He said also, "That old Dutchman was made in Cincinnati." "How could that be?" I asked. "Easily enough," he answered. "There was a factory there, a long building with partitions between the different sections and a chute that ran clear through the building. When they wanted to make a Dutchman, they took a hog and threw him in the chute at the front door. When he came to the last section of the building, they gave him a feed of sauerkraut and turned him loose a full-fledged Dutchman."

That night I happened to look up at the engine room and saw someone standing on the boiler with a bucket in

41

his hand. I got up and walked over in that direction and when I got close, I saw that it was Crawford. He had raised the beam and was pouring something into the boiler.

I asked him what he was doing and he said, "Old Bill has a ticket for the moon and I am going to help him off. When they raise steam again, this molasses that I am pouring in here will foam up so that he will think there is water in the boiler when there will be none, for I am going to bore a hole in the lead pipe going into the well so that none can go in when the pump is working. The check valve will make the same sound as it makes when there is water in the boiler. I would like to see Bill when he gets to the moon." That night Crawford left and I never saw him again.

A few days after he left, they raised steam again. As I was going to the slaughterhouse to get some meat to cook for dinner, having entirely forgotten about the Crawford episode, I passed the engine house and glanced up at the meter, I saw that it was in about the same condition as it was at the time of my first firing experience, when I came very nearly blowing up the works.

I remembered what Crawford had done to the boiler and pump and, calling Bill, I told him that he had better let off steam at once or the whole works would blow up. He refused to believe me until he saw me run off a couple of hundred yards, after which he began letting off steam.

When I came back and told him all that Crawford had done, he said, "You ought to be put in the penitentiary for not telling me sooner."

Old Bill was a curious character. He was subject to morose spells that would last for days, while at other times he would be in the best humor.

After Crawford left, I decided that I would leave as soon as my month was up, as Bill had offered me nothing extra for my night work. The night before the expiration of my time, Bill seemed to be in the best spirits that I had ever seen him in. I therefore determined to question him in regard to the factory in Cincinnati. I said to him, "Bill, were you ever in Cincinnati?" "Sure," he answered, "were you?" "No," I replied. "Why do you ask?" said Bill. "Crawford told me," I answered solemnly, "that you were made in Cincinnati. That there was a factory there, where they threw in a hog and brought out a Dutchman."

With this Bill got so angry that he turned white as a sheet and stood for a moment as if paralyzed. He reached for the top of a pile of wood and took a four-foot chunk and drew it back as if to strike me, saying, "Did you believe that dirty . . . ?" "No," I answered, "it was not I who said it, it was Crawford."

Bill was so angry that he shook his head as if he had the palsy. The next morning I resigned. Bill afterwards moved his packery to Flour Bluff, stayed there a few months and then moved to Padre Island where he finally went bankrupt.

Murder at Hall's Packery — During my last stay at Rockport, a brutal murder occurred. A man by the name of Toomey, who worked in the packery, lived a couple hundred yards from the slaughterhouse. Among those working at the packery was one named George French and another man by the name of Fitzpatrick. It seems that the man Toomey had forbidden these two men to go to his house, which was on the side of a hill.

One Sunday, a group of men, including French and Fitzpatrick, were assembled at the foot of the hill fronting Toomey's house. They were amusing themselves running burro races and with other games. Later in the evening they all left except French and Fitzpatrick, who stretched out on the grass to talk.

In the meantime, Toomey, who had been drinking heavily all day, spotted them and walked down to where they were. He commenced a friendly conversation with them and ended by telling them that if they ever needed a friend, to be sure and call on him. They thanked him and assured him that they would.

Toomey picked up a piece of pine scantling about five feet long. With this he struck French in the head, killing him instantly, and before Fitzpatrick could rise from the ground he killed him also.

Toomey Asks Advice — The murderer walked down to the American Beef Packery and told the boss butcher, whose name was Pat Connelly, what he had done and asked for his advice. Toomey was a Free Mason and so was Connelly. Thinking Toomey was drunk and blowing off, Connelly told him to go home and go to bed.

Death of the Murderer — By that time the bodies of the two men had been found and when Toomey reached his house a butcher by the name of Bob Stafford emptied a six-shooter at him as he was entering the door. However, he didn't hit him. At that time there was a man by the name of Ed Harney[24] and his wife and child stopping with Toomey; Toomey would not let them leave the house. In a few moments, the house was surrounded by the employees from the three packeries who fired shots at the murderer every time they could get a glimpse of him. Sometime after midnight, one of the mob threw a stick of wood and broke a window, after which he slipped up and shot Toomey

---

[24] Edward Harney was the grandfather of John B. Harney, the later sheriff of Nueces County. Edward managed a packery at Fulton and later at Nuecestown.

through the breast. Just before daybreak Toomey gave up the ghost.

CHAPTER FIVE

WITH THE TEXAS RANGERS

I Join Chamberlain's Company — Shortly after I left Bill's employ, a man by the name of Bland Chamberlain came to Corpus Christi for the purpose of organizing a company of Texas Rangers. He had a commission from the government to do so. My brother Matt and I joined the company and found it the worst mixed lot of men that ever came together in one organization.

Out of the company of sixty men there were but five Texans: L. Daughtrey, William O. Nieland, Willey Nickels,[25] Matt Dunn and myself. There were eight Mexican members, a Mississippi man named Oliver, and one of Quantrill's ex-guerrillas named Gus Pool. The rest of the company were fished out of the slums in San Antonio by the first sergeant, John Morgan, with the exception of Billie Cline, the bugler, who was from Louisiana, and a Frenchman who had been a member of Maximilian's army in Mexico.

The man Morgan was an ex-sergeant in the Union army and was a regular brute. He tried to enforce the same tactics in the ranger service as he had been accustomed to in the regular army. In recruiting for the company, he invariably tried to get all the ex-regular soldiers that he could to

---

[25] The name was probably Nichols. Dunn was very casual about spelling names. In one case, he refers to "Jose" as "Hosa."

strengthen his personal influence and he succeeded. While in camp on the Salado he brought in some of the most dilapidated, diseased, moth-eaten specimens of humanity that I have ever seen. Some of them could not stay on a trotting horse without holding on to the timber knocker, as they called the pommel of the saddle.

A Leaf from Morgan's Past — Just after the Civil War, Morgan's company was stationed at Gonzales. While there, one of his men abused a Dr. Cunningham who lived in Gonzales. When Morgan heard of it, he took a file of soldiers and followed the doctor to the Keyser House. As Morgan and his men arrived the doctor was going up the steps of the hotel to his room. Morgan called to him to halt at the same time telling his men to fire, which they did, killing the doctor immediately. This was during the Reconstruction days when the country was under carpetbag rule and a Southern citizen's life was not worth much.

We were out about nine months when we were ordered to disband.

Fate of Morgan — Since writing the above, I have learned that Morgan later went to Mexico and tried to force his tactics on the Mexican people. They put him in the penitentiary and when he attempted to escape they shot him to death. It is a blessing that the soil of Texas was not contaminated by drinking his blood.[26]

The Fight at Beeville — While on our way to Austin to be disbanded, we camped one night at Beeville on the south

---

[26] Dunn may be wrong about Morgan's fate. John Wesley Hardin, while in prison, pled guilty to killing John B. Morgan, a former Ranger and former deputy of Jack Helm in the State Police force, on April 4, 1873, according to the "Sutton–Taylor Feud" by Chuck Parsons.

side of the creek. Morgan, knowing that every man in the company hated him, got the idea that they intended killing him before they got to Austin. So he went to the captain and told him a lot of lies and persuaded him to have a roll call at dark and to issue orders that no one should leave camp and that no one should bring whiskey into the camp.

As the boys knew the instigator of the scheme, it made them angry and some of them determined to go and get whiskey anyway. As soon as the roll was called and Sergeant Morgan read the orders, the second sergeant, a Texas boy named Willie Nickels, called Matt and me and told us to come with him. Thinking that perhaps we were detailed for some purpose, we went with him to town. He bought four bottles of whiskey and went back to camp, walking within ten feet of where the captain and Morgan and some Mexicans were sitting on a blanket playing cards.

The captain looked up and said, "What have you there, Nickels?" "Whiskey," answered the latter. "Were you not at the roll call?" asked the captain. Nickels said, "Yes, I was there and heard the orders, but I pay for my own whiskey and I am going to drink it." The captain replied, "All right, but I shall hold you responsible for anything that may happen."

It was getting dusk and Nickels walked over to where some of the boys were talking and gave them two bottles of the whiskey. In the meantime, Morgan assembled the ex-soldiers that were in the company and had been discharged out of the regular army. This band came over to where we were.

Morgan was a very strong man and he slipped up till he got behind Nickels and struck him on the back of the neck and knocked him up against a wagon. A man by the name of Pool, who had been one of Quantrill's guerrillas, struck Morgan with his gun and knocked him on all fours. With that, a fellow by the name of Oliver jumped astraddle of Morgan and drove his spurs into Morgan's flanks, which caused Morgan to buck like a bronco. He finally tore loose from Oliver, but dragged him several feet, as the latter's spurs had fastened in Morgan's clothes.

Morgan's Retreat — When Morgan did get loose, he went through space like a shooting star going straight toward the creek and passing his four partners who had already emigrated. As he ran by where the captain and the Mexicans were, the Mexicans grabbed the captain and followed suit. In the meantime Pool, who had knocked Morgan down, was right behind the latter, pumping the gun between his shoulders, not knowing that he had broken it when he struck Morgan first. With the disappearance of Morgan and his bunch, those who remained were in charge of the camp.

The men who had run away got into the creek. A system of sniping on both sides followed. About ten o'clock our bugler, who was full of booze, set fire to one of the company's wagons. This lit up the surrounding country and made good targets of us for the runaways to shoot at. In burning the wagon, all the company's papers were destroyed besides the officers' clothing and fancy grub.

A Flag of Truce — Shots were fired all through the night, but fortunately no one was hurt. Just before daylight, we persuaded Sergeant Nickels to mount his horse and leave, knowing that he would be held responsible for the whole trouble. As soon as day began to break, we saw the company doctor coming in a gallop, carrying a white flag. (Bear in mind that when the Mexicans ran away they took the captain with them and left their guns lying on the ground. We picked these up and stacked them against a tree.) The doctor told us that the captain had said that if we would return the guns, he would overlook the trouble, as it was nothing but a drunken row. We returned the guns and as soon as the Mexicans received them, most of the boys were sent out to hunt the horses that had escaped during the night.[27]

Five Men Are Put in Irons — As soon as they were gone, five of the boys were arrested, Gus Pool, Oliver, Daughtrey, the bugler and one whose name I have forgotten. They were all taken to a blacksmith shop and irons were riveted to their wrists and legs. Morgan stated that they would be tried for mutiny.

Flynn Goes Into Action — Our first lieutenant was known among us as Flynn, but that was not his name. He had had some trouble in lower California and was known there as Three-fingered Jack, as he had but three fingers on one hand. It was said that he fought his way from lower California to Matamoras, Mexico, having but four men out of the 82 who had accompanied him when he left California. Flynn was not with us when the trouble started. If he had been, not one of the boys would have been arrested. We were camped on Onion Creek this side of Austin when Flynn came into camp.

When he saw the boys in irons he asked the cause. He called Morgan and said, "Take the irons off those boys quick and handle them gentle!" Morgan started to say

---

[27] This episode is recounted in "The Texas Rangers: Wearing the Cinco Peso" by Mike Cox. He wrote that Bland Chamberlain's Company H spent a few months scouting the Rio Grande, that its service record amounted to only a few words, and that it was only the Ranger company known to have mutinied in the field.

something but Flynn told him to shut up or he would put a pair on him. The irons were removed.

We Have Another Engagement — We reached Austin on St. Patrick's day. We were so ragged that the officers were ashamed to take us into the city, so they put us in camp near the old Military Academy.

There was a brewery within a hundred yards of our camp. As we had no money, we pawned pistols and carbines and bought beer by the keg. In the meantime, some of the cadets from the Academy happened to stroll into our camp. We filled them up with beer and in a few minutes a large crowd of them arrived. Among them were two cadets from Gonzales County who had plenty of money. They sent a negro to town to get several bottles of whiskey. Then the fun began. In a short time, the place looked like a battlefield, with the cadets stretched out in their nice white uniforms and the rangers in their dirty rags. The Academy had to send an ambulance after their casualties that night.

We Are Disbanded — The next day we were marched to the old Capitol and were discharged. Some of the boys were so drunk that it took two sober ones to hold each of them up while waiting for their discharge.

We Get Cheated — After we got our discharges and part of our pay, we were given to understand that if certain ones of us would return to Santa Gertrudis and go into camp there, we would be sent commissions in a few weeks and be put on the State Police force that was being organized at that time. We were also told that we would be sent vouchers for the balance of our pay. Pool, Oliver, Hannigan and I went to Santa Gertrudis and worked for Captain King for three months, but we never heard anything about vouchers or commissions.

When we saw how badly we had been duped, we left Santa Gertrudis and scattered, hunting work. None of us ever met again. Heath joined another Ranger company in Red River County[28] and was killed in the first fight they had with the Indians there. Pool, Hannigan and Oliver, I never heard from again.

The Bull Incident — While we were camped near King Ranch an amusing thing occurred. It was customary in the morning at roll call to detail different squads of men for duty during the day. Among them there was a squad whose duty it was to drag wood into camp for the night, going out on horseback and dragging in the wood by the horns of the saddle. If the night was very cold, we would take a cord of wood and set it on fire all at once. It would warm the whole camp.

A couple of nights before, an old Mexican bull or work ox had been noticed slipping into the camp after everything had quieted down. He was seeking warmth and would lie down by the fire and sleep. This night he must have been very cold for he came into camp earlier than usual and sniffed around for a while and stretched out within four feet of where my bunky, John Heath, and myself were lying. We were awake and kept watching him dreaming and chewing his cud.

But his peace was destined to a rude disturbance for he had gotten too near the fire. When he felt the hot ashes and coals he went up into the air like a rocket, bellowing and snorting worse than a whale. In a few moments pandemonium broke loose.

---

[28] In North Texas, between Paris and Texarkana.

The Third Battle of Bull Run — Every man in camp was on his feet in a moment, shooting at every object that he could see. Some were considerably mashed up by the bull's sharp hoofs. Others ran out and climbed trees and hid in the chaparral, at least the Mexican members of the company did so. The darkness of the night made it still worse, as the bull went pitching and jumping through the firelight, scattering coals and ashes. In a few minutes some of the beds were on fire and we had a time putting them out. The next morning we took an inventory of our losses and they tallied as follows: Two broken saddles, one broken bridle bit, two wounded men, one broken shovel, one broken wagon tongue, one bullet-riddled saddle.

A Sensitive Guest — The Mexicans did not get in until nine o'clock. I cannot account for the fact that no one was killed unless there is truth in the theory that there is a special Providence that watches over fools and drunkards. One of the Mexicans who came in reported having seen the bull about three miles from camp. He had a bullet wound in one of his front legs and had been so badly scorched by the fire that he looked like a pictorial map of Mexico. He must have been a very sensitive animal for he never called again.

My Last Squirrel Hunt — Just after being mustered into service in Chamberlain's company in San Antonio, we went into camp on the Salado Creek, a few miles from town. One day a stranger rode into camp, tied his horse and went over to some of the boys and asked questions about the company.

While he was talking, one of our men walked over to where he was and began abusing him. The stranger told him that he did not want any trouble with him and mounted his horse and left camp. We asked Daughtrey, (the man who had abused the stranger) what the trouble was between them. Daughtrey stated that about two years before he and Sullivan (the stranger) happened to be drinking in the old town of San Patricio and that Sullivan had given him a terrible beating.

A few days after the above incident, Daughtrey said to me, "Let's go out and kill some squirrels." I agreed and we started out. When we were about two miles from camp, we came upon a small frame house in a bunch of live oaks. Daughtrey turned and rode toward the house, saying as he did so, "This is where that fellow Sullivan lives and I wanted you to stand by me."

I told him I wanted nothing to do with the trouble but he paid no attention to me. He rode up to the front door and called. A man came to the door and Daughtrey asked him if Sullivan was there. He told him that he was Daughtrey and that he wanted to see Sullivan, and the man, whose name was Brady, called the latter, who came out. Daughtrey asked him if he was as anxious to fight as he was the other day in camp. Sullivan answered that he was not anxious to fight but that if he were driven to it he would do his best.

The Women Take A Hand — Daughtrey told him to come on away from the house and they would settle the matter. With that Brady came to the door and said, "There is not going to be any fighting around here." At the same time, he turned to one of his daughters in the house and said to her, "Get my hat, I am going to San Antonio and have that company moved away from here." His daughter handed him a seven-shot Spencer carbine while at the same time his wife and two daughters jumped in front of him and he began yelling and shooting over their shoulders at us.

I never pulled my pistol but Daughtrey did, at the sametime telling the women to get from in front of Brady or take the consequences. "No damn woman," he said, "is going to get between me and a man when I am fighting." He leveled his pistol at one of the women, but I knocked it down and the ball went into the fork of the saddle.

One of the Spencer bullets cut a limb off a mesquite tree and it fell squarely over my shoulders and hung there. I let it stay. I had no particular use for it, but it was more convenient to take it along than to lose time taking it off. We suddenly decided that discretion was the better part of valor and took a hurried departure. I was glad when we could no longer hear the whine of those Spencer balls that sounded the requiem of my last squirrel hunt.

CHAPTER SIX

UP THE TRAIL TO KANSAS

A Job with Martin Allen — After Pool, Hannigan, Heath, Oliver and myself started for northern Texas, we tried to find a herd of cattle that were going up the trail, hoping to find a job. Since every herd seemed well supplied with hands, I got disgusted and returned to Corpus. There I went out to what is now called the Roark farm,[29] a place at which a man by the name of Martin Allen was running a slaughterhouse, killing cattle for their hides and tallow. I worked for him about two months until he closed his slaughterhouse and bought two herds containing twelve hundred cattle each.

We Take the Trail — We started early in March. When we arrived at what was known as the Mustang Pens in Williamson County, the two herds were sold to the Avery brothers of Brushy in Williamson County. Some of the boys turned back when the herd was sold but I went on with the herd to Fort Hays, Kansas, now called Hays City.

We had a very nice trip. After crossing the Red River into the Indian Nation we found plenty of buffalo, elk, deer and

---

[29] James Henderson Roark owned a cabbage farm west of town at the turn of the 20th Century. He was called the largest truck farmer in Texas because he stood 6-4 and weighed 388 pounds.

antelope. In fact, we lived on the meat of these animals until we reached Fort Hays.

I Take Up Surgery — Just before we crossed the Red River, I performed my first surgical operation. We had a Mexican vaquero named Gregorio with us. One day the boss bought a large clumsy looking horse from a man that we met on the trail. He turned the horse over to Gregorio who saddled him at once and proceeded to rope a stray cow that had gotten into the herd. He roped the cow with the first throw of the rope and pulled on the reins to steady the horse.

He had a long rawhide lariat and when the cow had run its full length, the horse, instead of bracing himself, gave way and fell to the ground. Gregorio was winding the lariat around the horn of the saddle when the horse gave way and his hand got caught between the neck of the saddle and the rope. The horse lay there and grunted while the cow jumped up and began jerking and pulling on the rope. This ground Gregorio's fingers into shreds before one of the boys could get there and cut the rope.

He was so weak that we had to carry him into camp and pour water on him. We were a hundred miles from a doctor and someone remarked that the fingers and some of the loose flesh that was hanging from his arm and hand should be taken off. But no one would volunteer to do it.

Finally, I decided to do it myself and placed a cracker box alongside the wagon tongue and had him sit on it and made him lean his elbow on the tongue of the wagon. One man sat on the tongue and another sat on the box beside him and held an arm around him to steady him. I got my razor and cut off his fingers and all the loose skin that was hanging in shreds from his wrist and hand. Afterwards, I dug a hole and buried them. We made a poultice of cornmeal mush and let it cool and wrapped his hand up in it.

While near the Red River we came to a farm and Mr. Avery made arrangements with the farmer to take care of him, leaving him all that was due him and other money besides. That was the last we ever heard of Gregorio.

I Take Chills and Fever — After we rested the herds for a few days at Fort Hays, they started them for Nebraska. As all the Texas boys were quitting, so did I. When I left Fort Hays, I went to St. Louis, Mo., then across the Mississippi River into Illinois where I contracted the ague. I used to have chills so severely that my teeth would snap like those of a javelina. While we were coming down the Mississippi, I would crawl under the boilers trying to keep warm but it was impossible. It reminded me of a yarn that I had heard a fellow tell about the Brazos River in Texas. He said that the malaria was so bad there that the alligators would crawl out when they saw a passerby and ask him for a dose of quinine. A bullfrog would jump on top of a log and cry out, "Double the dose, double the dose!"

At St. Louis I engaged passage on the steamboat "T. M. McGill." The whole crew with the exception of the captain and the first and second mates were negroes and they let no opportunity pass to curse and abuse white passengers. One day one of them abused a young white man without any cause. There were two other white men with him but they were powerless to help him, knowing that if they even opened their mouths all the negroes would jump on them and perhaps hack them to pieces with razors.

Serious Consequences — A day or so after the above incident, one of the crew came running from the wheelhouse with a bloody hat in his hand, crying out,

"Somebody has been killed on this boat." It was some time before they could determine the ownership of the hat, but finally it was recognized by its former owner who had traded it to the negro who had abused the boy. The boy had slipped up on his tormentor and killed him in the wheelhouse, where he went through into the river.

When he struck the negro he threw the bar into the wheelhouse but one of the paddles caught it and threw it back. The boys were never molested again and all was quiet on the Mississippi.

A Strange Bedfellow — We were towing two large barges destined for Cairo, Ill. One night on waking from sleep I thought that we had arrived at that place. Accordingly, I stepped ashore and went into a saloon. Just as I did, I heard the boat backing out. My valise was on board and my passage was paid to New Orleans. I asked the barman what place it was and he told me that it was Cape Girardeau, Mo., and that was the only hotel in the place. He also stated that if I stayed all night I would have to occupy a bed with another man, and pointed to an individual seated on a bench in the saloon.

I did not like the looks of my prospective bedfellow. I went upstairs and took my money, which was in a flat leather pocketbook, and laid it on top of one of the bed slats under the mattress. I went to bed.

When my roommate came up, he said, "Are you asleep, partner?" I pretended to be asleep and said nothing. He made a systematic search, feeling all over me and giving me the same sensation as if he had been a rattlesnake. I was powerless to help myself. Between him and the bedbugs I passed a horrible night, for the latter pests simply came in swarms.

Sometime before, I had heard a fellow tell about getting in the same predicament. He described how he had fought valiantly against the bedbugs until he could struggle no longer and finally fell into a deep slumber. He dreamed that he was awakened by the sweetest music he had ever heard and believed he had arrived at the Pearly Gates and that the angels were coming to escort him.

Now, in his previous combat with the bugs, he would catch a handful of them and, lighting a match, throw both the bugs and the lighted match into a bucket of water at the side of his bed. When he heard the singing, he sat up, trying to locate it, and finally decided that it was at the side of his bed. He lit a match and looked down. He saw that the bedbugs had built a raft out of the stumps of the matches and were floating around in the bucket singing, "A life on the ocean wave, and a home in the rolling deep!"

I Catch Up with the Boat — The next morning I went down to the levee and found a little sternwheeler called the "Champion." I asked the captain how far down the river he was going and he told me he was bound for Cairo. I took passage with him, never dreaming we would catch up with the "T. M. McGill" which had been traveling all night, but we passed her and got into Cairo four hours ahead of her.

A Fight at the Landing — The next day our smart negro crew got smashed up in grand style. We were taking on freight at a small landing on the river. The warehouse was some four or five hundred yards from the river and the elevation was so high that they could put a barrel of flour on a track that led from the door and give the barrel a shove that would make it roll like lightning down to the boat. In about 20 feet of the boat this track had been broken by high water and a negro had to stand by the broken place and steady the barrel with his hand. Otherwise, when the barrel came to the broken place, it would jump the track. Some of the crew tried to take a watermelon from a white boy on the levee and the negro that was watching the barrel turned his head to see the row. When the barrel came in, it struck the broken place, jumped the track and, striking the negro square in the mouth, broke his jaw and knocked out his front teeth.

On deck and at the foot of the track there was also a crowd of negroes stationed to catch and steady the barrels, while others stowed the barrels in the hold of the vessel. The next barrel that came down knocked two negroes off the deck, breaking one's shinbone and nearly drowning the other.

A Yellow Fever Scare — When I arrived at New Orleans, I found a Morgan steamer called the "Hutchinson." I boarded her for Galveston. A few hours after landing there, a man came in a great hurry to the hotel where I was stopping, and asked if anyone had ever had the yellow fever. I told him that I had had it in Corpus Christi in '67. He begged me to go with him and look at a man who was supposed to be suffering from that malady. I accompanied him and found that all the man had was cramps. I told him so, but before night all the back country had quarantined against Galveston.[30]

I Decide to Leave Town — Late that evening I heard that a locomotive and a caboose were going to be allowed to leave the city so that Gov. E. J. Davis, who was in

---

[30] Such a quarantine was bad news for the merchants since almost all commerce, especially with outlying towns, virtually ceased. Merchants and civic leaders would go to great lengths to keep the alarming news of a yellow fever outbreak from spreading.

Galveston at that time, might return to the capital. I went to the causeway and waited for the train to come along, knowing it would cross slowly.

On arriving there, I was surprised to find two of the young fellows who were supposed to have been implicated in the killing of the negro on the boat bound for New Orleans. They told me they were going to ride the ladders across and showed me how to manage it.

We reached Houston all right, but it was like jumping from the frying pan into the fire, as all the towns were quarantined against Houston also. The next night I slipped out of Houston on foot, trying to make Gonzales where I had a horse.

Getting Out of Houston — I got along pretty well until I came to Columbus. The night was pitch dark and I had to cross a long railroad bridge, carrying my heavy valise. There was no footbridge. I had to straddle the rails carrying my valise in one hand. Several times I almost fell through the trestle.

When I approached the opposite bank, I noticed a dim light in front of me and on drawing nearer I saw that it came from a tent made of very thin canvas through which I could see the shadows of two men playing cards. I had to shift myself to the other side of the railroad track and almost fell through, but eventually I got across. I hid my valise in a lumberyard and mixed in with a bunch of section hands who were going to a saloon. I stepped in ahead of them and asked them to have a drink, which they willingly did. I had had nothing to eat the day before, as I had run out of change and had nothing with me but ten- and twenty-dollar bills. Treating the crowd gave me plenty of change to take me to Gonzales.

I Encounter a Rube — My last adventure on this trip was at a place called East Bernard. It was a place in the midst of the prairie containing only a section house and a small country store. As I was burning up with thirst, I ventured into the store and asked the young rube who ran it for a drink of water. He told me that there was a well outside. After drinking, I went back inside and by that time four or five country girls had come into the store. No doubt the rube wanted a chance to display his intelligence before the girls, so he said to me, "Where are you from?" "From Richmond," I replied. "Is thar einy yaller fever thar?" he asked. I told him that I had not heard of any. "Did you ask permission before you came up here?" he continued. I told him that I did not since I had met nothing but three head of cattle since leaving Richmond.

In a side room there were several cowboys who were regaling themselves on some bottled beer. He turned to one of them and said, "What became of that fellow who came here the other day without asking permission?" I answered before anyone else could, telling him that I had seen the man in a gully and that he had sent a message I did not care to repeat. With that the cowboys came in and filled me up on beer, and among us all we gave him a racket. I told him that I guessed I had been in Texas as long as he had. He explained that the reason he had spoken to me the way he had was because he thought I was a damn Yankee.

After leaving the store, I returned to where I had cached my valise. A section boss and two hands came along in a handcar. The boss said, "Where are you going, young fellow?" "To Gonzales," I answered. "Jump up, young man," he told me, "and give us a hand and we will take you down to the end of the section." That was the only ride I got between Houston and Gonzales.

An Unlucky Venture — After I arrived at Gonzales, my brother Matt came there and we put in a crop of cotton and corn. My uncle, who owned the land, boarded the teams and was to give me half the crop. That fall an overflow came and washed most of it away. When we figured up our accounts we found that I had had the chills and fever nine months out of the twelve for my share and that my uncle had paid the expenses for his share. We were disgusted and let what was left of the crop go and went to San Antonio where we worked for the Ross brothers, who had a contract to furnish troops in San Antonio with hay for their horses. After finishing this job, we went to Leon Springs and cut hay in the canyons there, then went on to Culebra Springs[31] and other places that I have forgotten.

The German and the Indian — While we were at Culebra Springs, a traveler came into our camp and related an incident that had happened just three days before, about halfway between our camp and Castroville. It was the full of the moon and the Indians were known to be on one of their horse-stealing expeditions.

The traveler stated that just before sundown, a German peddler drove up to the farmhouse where he was stopping and asked the farmer if he could camp in the horse lot. The farmer told him that he could and also invited him to come inside after he had fed his horses and eat supper with him, saying also that he would furnish him a bed. The peddler thanked the farmer and told him that he would prefer to sleep in his wagon, as he understood that the Indians were in and that they might attempt to steal his horses.

---

[31] Dunn may have been referring to Culebra Creek in western Bexar County.

About midnight, the farmer heard a shot out at the lot and called to the peddler but could get no answer. He called several times with the same result, and concluded that the peddler had been killed.

The family, feeling sure that the Indians were around, sat up until daybreak watching the lot. When it became light enough to see they observed the peddler leaning over a hog pen, looking at the hogs. The farmer called to him and asked him what he had shot at. "Come and see," he answered.

When the farmer got there he saw the body of an Indian in the hog pen being eaten by the hogs. The German told him that as he lay awake watching his horses he observed the Indian slip up and commence to cut the rope of one of the horses, whereupon he emptied both barrels of buckshot into the prowler, and in order to dispose of the body he gave it to the hogs.

Two days after that, two men started to our camp but got lost and staked their horses out, placing their saddles for pillows against the bushes that the stake rope was tied to. When they awoke next morning, their horses were gone and they came into camp with their saddles on their shoulders. The Indians had cut their horses loose and stolen them. It seemed that the Indians were averse to killing anyone in those days if they could make a raid and get away with horses.

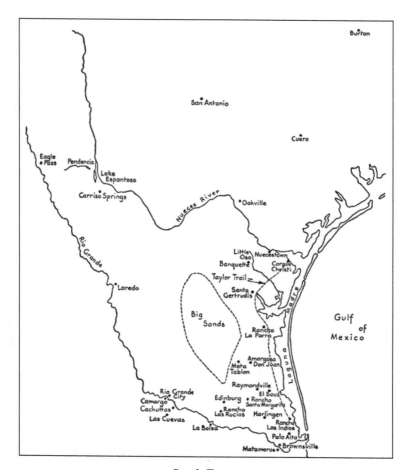

South Texas

CHAPTER SEVEN

A HORRIBLE CRIME

The Robbery and Murder at Peñascal — The following account of this horrible crime was published in the *Corpus Christi Gazette* as follows: "On the evening of the 15th. of May 1874, a bunch of armed Mexicans rode up to the Peñascal Ranch[32] and began shooting at everyone in sight, according to the Mexican cook who was returning from the well with a bucket of water. He first saw Mr. Tilgner running from the store vomiting blood, and saw him dispatched by the murderers, after which they shot Michael Morton four times through the head. Mr. Coakley was tied face down and three bullets fired into his body.

"The murder of John Morton, judging from circumstantial evidence, is beyond the power of man to describe. With deliberate coolness he was wounded so as to render him incapable of defending himself. In this condition he was forced to overhaul the goods in the store and deliver all valuables to the murderers. He was reserved for the last. From the position in which he was found it is believed that he [pleaded] on bended knees for his life. He was shot six times and when found was lying on his back near the counter with one leg bent under him and his prayer book lying by his side. The shelves, boxes and everything

---

[32] It was a one-store community on Baffin Bay, 50 miles south of Corpus Christi.

were covered with his blood. After completing their hellish work, the murderers got beastly drunk and remained in the house until nearly daylight. They loaded their horses with all the goods they could carry and left."

The Murderers Are Pursued — When the news reached town, several posses were immediately organized under different heads to capture the murderers. On leaving town, the pursuers took with them a Mexican by the name of Tom Basquez. He was a member of the city police and according to the testimony of the two murderers after their capture was the man who had originated and engineered the whole plot.

At that time, my brother Matt and I were living on the old homestead four miles west of Corpus Christi. When we learned that the posses had returned and had failed to capture the murderers, we decided to make an attempt of our own. We went to see John and Mike Dunn and held a council. Our decision was that we would go in different directions and see if we could strike a trail.

After dark we started in a northerly direction, crossing the Nueces River at Borden's Ferry and arriving at Mean's Village[33] just as day was breaking. We went to the house of a Mr. Britten Means and inquired if any strange Mexicans had passed there during the last day or so. He stated that he had seen none himself but would ask his Mexican helper. The Mexican stated that he had seen several who were hunting work as sheepherders and that since then he had seen some of them in a vacant jacal[34] about a mile away. Mr. Means now woke his brother, Paul, and they went with us.

---

[33] Meansville was a small ranching community established by the Means family in San Patricio County.

[34] Spanish for a crude brush hut, usually with a thatched roof.

We Follow the Clue — We surrounded the jacal and closed in on it just as daylight came, but it was empty and showed no signs of recent occupancy. After eating some breakfast, we started out again. We were just emerging from the heavy timber through which we had been riding and had started to enter the prairie when we spied a man on horseback coming out of the timber on the other side of the prairie from where we were.

We dropped back into the timber out of his sight and he started straight toward us. We sent two men, one on each side, to ride down through the timber and when they saw he was about halfway to us they were to strike a gallop and fall in behind him.

When the man got close to us he started to ride out to meet us, but immediately afterwards wheeled his horse to run. However, when he saw the two men behind him, he rode up to us.

We asked him where the Mexicans were and he answered that he did not know. One of the boys stuck a cocked sharpshooter rifle to his ribs and asked him again. Under this persuasion he stated that they were about two miles away in a sheep pen about eight feet high. There were thirty of them, he told us, and they would fight. He also mentioned that there were three strangers among them who had arrived a few days before.

On receiving this information we rode about a mile down the timber, then entered the timber that the Mexicans were in and found and surrounded the pen. It was just twelve o'clock and they were all sound asleep. The hard south wind had blown the big gate open and we charged right in among them before they knew we were there.

John Dunn and I happened to dismount from our horses right beside a blanket where two men were asleep. One of these, as we learned later, was Hypolita Tapia and the other

71

was Andres Davila, the two murderers. When we jerked the cover off Hypolita Tapia's head, he reached under his head and jerked out a moral.[35] I struck him across the forehead with my pistol and jerked the morral out of his hand. His pistol was in it. I still have the weapon in my possession.

Tapia fell on his knees before John Dunn and began begging him to spare his life. The murderer had once worked for John and knew him well.

After satisfying ourselves that these men were the only ones implicated in the murder and robbery, we took them back to Mean's Village.

When we arrived there it was dark and we placed the prisoners in a vacant room under guard. First we took Hypolita out and told him that we wanted him to tell us all about the murder but he stated that he would confess nothing. We took him to a tall mesquite tree and let him kick a few chunks out of the horizon, after which he stated that he was ready to divulge everything.[36]

We took Tapia back and put him in a separate room from that in which his companion was confined, after which we went and got Davila. When we got him outside the house, he asked us what we were going to do with him and we told him that all we wanted was a confession. He stated that he was ready any time we were and we returned him to his room and took Tapia before Mr. Direc Rachel,[37] who wrote down Tapia's confession and later that of Davila's, which corresponded with that of Tapia in every detail.

---

[35] Spanish for a nose bag carried on the saddle horn, usually filled with extra feed for the horse.

[36] Dunn was referring to a simulated hanging that was stopped short of being fatal.

[37] He was Darius C. Rachal, a prominent cattleman from the White Point area. His name was often mispronounced as "Direese."

Confessions of Hypolita Tapia and Andres Davila — After being sworn, Tapia was told to go ahead and tell everything that had happened from the beginning of the affair to the end. His confession was substantially as follows: "My name is Hypolita Tapia. I was born in Texas and am a vaquero and sheepherder. The first that I heard of the contemplated murder was from a Mexican by the name of Tellisfero Aguilar with whom I am well-acquainted. Aguilar is a brother-in-law of Tomas Basques who is a member of the police force of Corpus Christi.

"Aguilar came to me and told me that Basquez was in Mr. Buckley's store that morning where he stated that he had found out that there was a large consignment of goods and considerable money going to Peñascal in the evening, and that he wanted to raise ten men to go down and get it. I agreed to do this and secured the following men to join me, Andres Davila, an American called Joe,[38] Teodoro Aguilar, Pancho Luna, Antonio Martinez, Amado Lerma, a man called Octaviano and another called Chimito. When we arrived at Peñascal we noticed that the boat, on which the goods had been shipped, was lying out some distance from the shore. Therefore we supposed that the boat had landed the money and the goods."

At this point Mr. Rachel began to question the prisoner:

QUESTION: "Were you mistaken in thinking this?"

ANSWER: "Yes."

"What did you do next?"

"We surrounded the store and after shooting one man who was outside, we went inside and asked for the money."

---

[38] He was Joseph Delera. He had served in the U.S. Army under the name of Joseph Shane and was known on the border as "Jose el Americano." He was arrested in Matamoros by the Brownsville police and "met some sort of accident" on the way to Corpus Christi. From "Empresarios' Children" by Bill Walraven.

"Did they offer any resistance?"

"No, sir."

"Then why did you shoot them?"

"We told them to give us the money and they denied having any except what was in the drawer."

"How much was in the drawer?"

"Only $12 or $13."

"Then what did you do?"

"We commenced shooting them."

"Isn't it a fact that you shot some of them through the arms and then made them take goods from the shelf after doing so?"

"Yes."

"Who was the last man killed?"

"John, they called him."

"In what position was John when you killed him?"

"He was on his knees praying."

"What did you do after killing them?"

"We loaded the horses with things from the store and left."

"Why did you not go to Mexico instead of coming here?"

"I knew that they were shearing sheep and thought I could mix with the shearers without anyone finding out that I had been implicated in the murder and besides I knew that Basquez would keep me posted."

By the time that Mr. Rachel had finished writing these confessions, a crowd of ranchers had gathered around the place and wanted to hang the murderers at once. But John and Mike Dunn would not agree to it, stating that if they were hung it would destroy all the evidence against Basquez.

It was agreed by everybody that we would take the murderers back to Corpus Christi. We did so that night and turned them over to the sheriff.[39] A reward had been offered for them but it was never tendered to us and we never asked for it.[40]

The names of the murdered men were John Morton, Michael Morton, P. F. M. Coakley and Herman Tilgner.

The following was all that appeared in the Gazette after the capture of the murderers: "Three of the Peñascal murderers have been captured and locked in our jail. We presume the balance will be along in good time. Two parties of men are in search of them, one under Pat Whalen and the other under Bill Rhew." That was all the credit we received through the papers for the capture of the murderers. Tapia and Davila were hung in Corpus Christi.[41]

Hypolita's Brothers Swear Vengeance — After the capture of Tapia and Davila, it seemed as though we were going to have a spell of quiet for awhile. Consequently, all the boys except me scattered out to work. I remained alone on the old homestead. At night I would go over to my

---

[39] Sheriff John McClane.

[40] The reward offered by the Committee of Public Safety was $100 for the "Mexicans" and $250 for the "American named Joe."

[41] Besides Tapia and Davila, five other Mexican-Americans were arrested in connection with the crime, but they were not implicated. Threats were made by some to burn down Corpus Christi and free the prisoners. A new "Executive Committee of Public Safety" patrolled the streets around the jail to prevent a surprise attack. Davila and Tapia were executed by hanging on Aug. 11, 1874, less than three months after the murders at Peñascal. The week following the hanging, the Corpus Christi newspaper reported: "A ridiculous story was in circulation last Monday, to the effect that Davila, who was hanged last Friday, came to life and was seen riding through town. He was the 'deadest' man ever seen in these parts Friday evening; and a very grave subject to joke upon, his neck being completely broken." From the Nueces Valley, Aug. 15, 1874.

uncle's, a mile distant, and remain until I got sleepy, after which I would return home.

One night as I was on my way home I met one of my uncle's daughters and her husband coming home from a neighbor's. They stopped me and told me to turn back as there were a bunch of men in a large gully that I would have to cross. I went back to my uncle's with them. At daylight, I went to the crossing and found horse tracks and the butts of cigarettes. I knew something was brewing.

I heard that day that two of Hypolita's brothers had gotten in from the river and were swearing vengeance. That night after dusk, I took my sharpshooter and pistol and hid in a corn patch about 30 feet from the house. At the house, I had four vicious dogs that I knew would warn me if anyone prowled around. About 12 o'clock, I got thirsty and went into the house to get a drink of water. Up to this time, the dogs had not barked. I slipped in quietly and went to a table where there was a bucket of water with a dipper in it. When I put the dipper to my mouth, I thought I felt something in it. So I put the dipper down and, without thinking, struck a match and lit the lamp.[42]

I'm Attacked — No sooner had I done this than there was an explosion that put the lamp out. At first I thought the lamp had exploded. It was so dark that I could not find the doors. I could feel a stinging on my face and hands and could smell blood, and at last I realized that a shot had been fired. The dogs began to bark. I began calling the boys by name so that the prowlers would hear me and think that a number of us were there. The thought struck me that they might fire the house so I jerked the door open and crawled

---

[42] This story is told in "A Vaquero of the Brush County" but mistakenly identifies Matt Dunn, John's brother, as the one who was shot at.

to the corner of the house and squatted there. I could see no one. The night was as black as Egypt. I heard a big laugh and knew that the prowlers thought they had hit me. I opened fire on them but it was too dark to see anything.

It was only two days after this that I joined Wallace's company of Rangers.[43] While a member of that force, I had the opportunity of again meeting these nocturnal friends of mine and we arranged everything satisfactorily. The debt has been paid in full with interest.

Afterwards, I found that the shots were fired from two Winchester carbines. One of the shots did not get inside, but buried itself in the window frame. The other came through the center of the window pane, through my vest and struck the glass bowl of the kerosene lamp. The pieces from the lamp cut my face and hands.

---

[43] Following the Peñascal killings, Gov. Richard Coke, on June 18, 1874 authorized Warren W. Wallace to raise a company of 50 men "for the protection of all the counties below the lower Nueces and Rio Grande." It was this company, part of the newly created Frontier Battalion, that Dunn joined.

CHAPTER EIGHT

WITH WALLACE'S COMPANY

Trouble with Mexicans — After leaving the Ross brothers in San Antonio, my brother Matt and I returned to Corpus Christi. Shortly after we arrived, it seemed as if all the hell in the Mexican race had broken loose. The country was overrun with Mexican cattle- and horse-thieves as well as cutthroats.

In the lower country called the Sand thousands of heads of cattle belonging to the stockmen were killed and their hides sold to American merchants who boldly built stores for the purpose of disposing of the stolen goods.

I Join the Rangers Again — Things finally came to such a pass that Warren W. Wallace was authorized to organize a company of men and chase the bandits into Mexico if necessary.[44] My brother James and I joined his company, which established its headquarters at the Mexican town of Concepcion.[45]

---

[44] Texas' Adjutant General William Steele issued instructions that the Rangers could cross the border "if by so doing you have a good prospect for the recovery of property belonging to citizens of this state" but that order was soon rescinded after the U.S. Department of Justice objected.

[45] Though Dunn calls Concepcion a "Mexican town," it was eight miles southwest of San Diego in Duval County.

In a short time we captured a number of troublesome Mexicans. We also discovered that most of the depredations were incited by renegade white men who were living among the Mexicans and were profiting by their crimes.

Sam the Renegade — There was one man among them, an American whom I shall call Sam, who eventually caused us a lot of trouble. When we first went to Concepcion he paid no attention to us. After a while he became very friendly with the captain and was around him all the time. One evening he came in late and went to the captain's quarters. Just at dusk we received orders to saddle up and were started in the direction of the Nueces River. Sam and the captain accompanied us.

The next morning we found ourselves at Lagarto and went into camp there. The first night we were there a Mexican circus came in and pitched its tent.

Suspicious Proceedings — Just before the performance began, while I was talking with the second lieutenant, Lark Ferguson,[46] Sam came along with the proprietor of the circus. They talked together for a few moments and turned and walked over to us.

Sam introduced Ferguson to the Mexican who was pretty well loaded with booze. The Mexican stepped back, saying, "So this is Elario, is it?" with which words he spat at

---

[46] Lark Ferguson was later dismissed from the Rangers over at least two questionable killings of Mexican-Americans. He was named as one of the participants in the Seeligson bank robbery on Aug. 24, 1876. He changed his name to Pete Spence and moved to Arizona where he gained a reputation for stagecoach robbery and murder. From "John B. Armstrong, Texas Ranger and Pioneer Ranchman" by Chuck Parsons and "200 Texas Outlaws and Lawmen" by Laurence Yadon.

Ferguson and began hissing at him. (Elario was Ferguson's name in Spanish.)

As Ferguson reached for his pistol, the Mexican threw his arms around him and threw him to the ground, at the same time reaching for a knife in his belt. Someone struck the Mexican across the back of the neck and laid him out for a while. His hands were tied.

As soon as the Mexican could walk, Ferguson told two of the Rangers to take the prisoner out to the racetrack and hold him under guard, as he intended to find out what all the trouble was about.

In a short time he called me, saying, "Come with me out to the racetrack and we'll find out what is the matter with that prisoner." When we got within twenty or thirty feet of him, he sprang and made a dash at Ferguson, who fired at him, striking him between the eyes. He put his foot on the Mexican's neck and fired two more shots into his head.

Next day his troupe buried him and packed up and left for Mexico. About a week afterwards, Ferguson and I were surprised to learn that the troupe had deposited a $1,000 reward for myself and Ferguson for $500 each.

After staying at Lagarto a few days, we went back to Concepcion, where we heard that the bandit Caballo Blanco[47] and his partner had made a big raid, taking hundreds of cattle and horses across the border.

At Concepcion we also heard a great deal about our trip to Lagarto. But something happened in a short time that caused us to forget the incident for the time being.

The Shooting of Mark Judd — One day, three or four of us left camp to go to town, that is, to the village of

---

[47] A notorious bandit and hide thief, Alberto Garza, was also called Caballo Blanco, White Horse.

Concepcion, which was about two miles from where we were stationed. On our way in we met two of our boys on their way back to camp. One of them was riding a racehorse that belonged to Lieutenant Ferguson. The rider, who was pretty full of booze, began wallowing around on his horse and talking very loud. His actions excited the horse and as the other horses also began moving, he thought it was a race that was coming off and wheeled and ran in the opposite direction, as fast as he could go. We knew it would only make matters worse if we tried to catch him, as this would only make him ride faster and he had the fastest horse in the company.

In a few moments both he and the horse disappeared in the chaparral and we rode on in the direction of Conception. When we got in sight of the captain's quarters, we saw the horse going there in a dead run, with the rider, Mark Judd, hanging over on the horse's shoulder. Both Judd and the horse were covered with blood.

When the horse halted at the door of the captain's quarters, we eased Judd down and saw that he had been shot in the eye with a small caliber pistol and that one side of his face was laid open with a machete. He was unconscious and could say nothing.

We got on the trail of the blood and followed it to a Mexican jacal where even the door was splattered with blood. We found no men within but only women and children who denied any knowledge of the affair.

The Fight at the Jacal — We threw guards around this jacal and several others in the vicinity until more of the boys came so that we could search the premises thoroughly.

Dave Odem,[48] Billie McKintosh, myself and one other guarded the first jacal to which we had trailed the blood.

We were in a vacant garden or path overgrown with tall weeds when I heard a noise behind me. I turned around and there, lying on his stomach, with a machete in his hand, was a Mexican. About ten feet from this one was another Mexican grasping a club of mesquite wood.

We captured and disarmed them and found that they had crawled about thirty yards toward us before we spotted them.

The one who had the machete had a mop of frizzy hair that looked more like a buffalo's mop than anything else. Right away one of the boys, whom we called Chubby Cody, named him Moss Top. The latter was in his shirt sleeves and his body was covered with awful sores from which the stench was terrible.

We lost no time in getting to camp with our prisoners. When we arrived there, a scout under Steve Burleson came in and asked us what we had with us. We told him the circumstances and he threw a noose around Moss Top's neck and began throwing the other end of the rope over a tree. Captain Wallace and some more of the boys came running up. At first, the captain tried to bluff the boys out of hanging the prisoner, but when that did not work, he gave them his word of honor as a gentleman that if they would desist he would keep him under guard until the grand jury was in session and would turn him over to the law.

---

[48] Dave Odem, a rancher, later became a longtime sheriff of San Patricio County, serving from 1883 to 1914. The town of Odem was named for him. From "History of San Patricio County" by Keith Guthrie.

The Captain Breaks His Word and Its Consequences — A few days later we learned that Moss Top had been liberated. The boys put spies on his track and found that at a certain time every evening he took a rope and his machete and went after wood to the creek.

The next day, the boys hid in a gully that ran into the creek and caught him easily. They made him mount behind one of them and tied his legs underneath the horse's belly so that if he happened to fall or jump, he could not escape.

They struck a run for a small lake in the mesquite brush which was surrounded by mesquite timber, but they could not find a tree large enough or high enough to swing him clear of the ground. After losing considerable time trying to find one, they sighted a tree that forked high enough from the ground to fasten his head in the forks and leave his toes about four inches from the ground. They jammed his head into the fork of the tree, took the end of the rope and put it around his neck and one of the forks of the tree. They tied the other end of the rope around the horn of the saddle and made the horse pull until the man's neck was broken. After this they removed the rope that they had used and tied him with his own rope.

He was not found for several days, and it was in the month of August; the weather was very warm and showery. Consequently, the body was a terrible sight, swollen beyond recognition and emitting a terrible odor.

The Mexicans pretended that they were afraid to take him down and the Rangers refused to do so, so they sent to Santa Gertrudis (King Ranch) for a detail to come and bury him.

Mark Judd, the man whom he had shot and stabbed, recovered, but he was blind in one eye and carried a scar from his hair down the side of his neck.

Lieutenant Ferguson and the Signal Man — The worst place for scouting that I ever saw was on the Frio River. There the chaparral and prickly pears were so dense that it was almost impossible to ride through them. I have seen prickly pears as tall as a man on horseback.

About the only living thing that one could see would be javelinas and rattlesnakes and the stench from both of them would keep the horses continually snorting. It was almost impossible to follow a trail, on account of the Mexican signal men who were posted on the summits of the high hills.

At this time we were on the trail of a Mexican bandit by the name of Alberto Garza, who had stolen a number of horses and was hiding in that section. We had been there several days but Garza's signal man kept him well posted and he gave us the slip.

One day Lieutenant Ferguson said to me, "I am going to get one of those birds this morning." He ordered the company to saddle their horses and be ready to move when wanted. He told them that if they heard two shots in succession to come in a hurry.

We rode toward a large hill, higher than the rest, and when we got about half way, we saw smoke curling up from it. We rode as fast as possible, following a dry gully that led near it and when we got close, Ferguson got off his horse and handed me the reins, telling me to follow slowly as he was going to try to slip up on the signal man.

Suddenly, I heard his sharpshooter boom. About the same time, he yelled, "Come on, I have got him." The signal man was as dead as a nail. The bullet had hit him in the neck, breaking it. We fired two shots and the rest of the boys came up. We found the man's old burro tied in the gully and turned him loose and also found a sack with old pieces of bootlegs, shoes, and a can of tallow used to color the smoke.

CHAPTER NINE

WITH WALLACE'S COMPANY, CON'T

Ferguson and the Dutchman — One day about noon, as we were going to strike camp, several of the boys with Lieutenant Ferguson started out to get a calf for meat. As there were no cattle in sight, they scattered in different directions to find them.

A few minutes after they parted, we heard some fast shooting in a certain direction and started in a run toward where the sound was coming from. When we got close enough, we saw Ferguson riding in circles and shooting at someone who was behind a tree shooting at him.

We gave a yell so that the lieutenant would know that help was at hand. When we were within a couple of hundred yards, we saw the man behind the tree fall over. Ferguson dismounted and raised up the man's head. He had been shot through the shoulder and his collarbone was broken.

It was a mistake on both sides. Each one had mistaken the other for Mexicans, since both were wearing large Mexican hats. The man who was shot was a Dutchman in the employ of a sheepman by the name of Staples.[49] The Dutchman had been in this country but a short time and did not

---

[49] W. W. (William Washington) Staples was a well-known rancher in Live Oak County. His brother Wayman N. Staples owned a grocery store in Corpus Christi. Staples Street was named for him.

understand the Mexican language, which Ferguson spoke to him. So he got excited and began shooting.

The tree behind which he had taken refuge was a very small one but Ferguson put three bullets in it. When he saw his mistake, he went to the ranch and got a wagon and team and sent the wounded man back to his employer. He recovered, but his neck was always crooked. Several times afterwards we ate dinner at the same ranch. It was comical to see how the Dutchman would look at Ferguson while waiting on the table where we were eating.

Trouble with the Mexican Pastores[50] — In Wallace's company it was a common occurrence to be called at any hour of the night for scout duty. On one particular occurrence there was no bread cooked in camp and it was so dark that the pack mule could not be found. We started for the Frio without anything to eat.

The next day we found a herd of goats and filled up on goat meat. We had received word that a bunch of horses had been stolen and had been seen to enter the brush near the Frio River.

After devouring the goat meat, we had nothing else to eat all day. That night at dusk we came to a small glade or opening in the chaparral with a small pond of muddy water. We dismounted and staked our horses, intending to remain there all night. The water was so muddy we had to take prickly pear leaves, cut the thorns from them and split the leaves, and drop them in the water to settle it.

The drought and hunger seemed to affect a boy named Chubby and myself more than anyone else in the company. As we were sitting on our blankets Chubby suddenly said to me, "Look, is that a star or a light?" I looked in the

---

[50] Sheepherders, or shepherds.

direction he pointed and saw a peculiar light. It would flame up for a second or so and then disappear and flame up again, seeming not to be over five hundred yards from us.

When we found that everybody was asleep, we slipped our saddles out to where our horses were staked, saddled the animals and struck out to investigate. After riding about a mile we came to the foot of a high hill, and could see that the light was right on top of it. We dismounted and climbed the hill on foot by crawling. When we got about halfway up, we stopped and formed the following plan:

If we found two in the camp we had discovered, Chubby was to crawl to the right hand man and jump astraddle of him and I was to do the same with the one on the left. As we drew near, we saw what was making the light. It was a side of mutton ribs broiling before the fire, and when the hot grease would drop on the fire it would blaze up and then die down until the next drop fell.

We rushed to the attack. I happened to control my man all right but Chubby did not have such good luck. His prisoner bucked like a bronco and, throwing Chubby over, escaped into the brush. Chubby fired three shots at him as he ran and we then began to feast on the mutton ribs.

We could hear the boys in camp firing guns and yelling through the brush for us, but we were too busy to answer and let them hunt until we had finished our feast, to the disgust of our prisoner.

We fired a few shots and let them find us, after which we went to the sheep pen which was within thirty steps of the captured camp and got several fine muttons, which we took to camp. We dressed and ate three of them before daylight. The taste of that mutton always comes back to me when I am hungry. I trust that the Frio country is better now than it was then. Adios, Frio.

Duel Between Buck Harris and Joe Osgood — Both Harris
and Osgood were members of Wallace's company. Osgood
was industrious and hard-working while Harris was exactly
the reverse. At roll call each morning, it was customary to
detail men for the day for various duties.

One morning Buck Harris had been detailed to bring in a
beef for meat. When notified, he pretended that he was sick
and refused to go. Joe Osgood offered to go and did so. In
half an hour he returned with a beef. He rode around a
mesquite tree and tying the rope to it, pulled out his pistol,
shot the beef and began to skin it.

He had it about one third skinned when Harris came
walking up to him. "What are you going to do, Buck?" said
Osgood. "I am going to cut myself a piece of meat," replied
Harris. "No, you are not," answered Osgood. "It was your
day to bring in the meat and you refused."

With that Buck Harris reached for his pistol and Joe
Osgood did likewise. They fired at the same time. Joe's ball
entered Buck's right arm below the shoulder, shattering it
to pieces while Harris's ball struck Joe squarely in the
middle of the pistol belt, going through four doubles of
leather, passing through his bladder and breaking his
hipbone to pieces.

When Osgood fell back, he rested on one hand and tried
to cock his pistol again, but it was a Smith and Wesson
with a very short hammer and his thumb would slip on it.

I ran to him and eased his head onto my thigh and he
said, "The ____ has got me, John." I said, "No, Joe, you
will be all right." But in a minute he was dead. Harris
recovered but his hand and arm shrank away to where it
was no larger than a child's.

If the tales that an older member of the company used to
tell on Buck Harris were true, he was certainly cold-
blooded. This man said that Harris had gone up the trail to

Kansas the year before. There was a youngster along of not over fourteen or fifteen years of age. One day while in camp in the Indian Nation the boss of the herd sent Harris and the boy over to a pond for a bucket of water. Sometime later, they heard a shot in the direction that the two had gone. They paid little attention, thinking they were shooting at prairie dogs.

They became uneasy as Harris and the boy did not return and sent a man out to look for them. In a few moments, the man returned, saying, "I see Buck coming now." The latter came into camp and set the bucket down. "Where is the boy?" they asked him. He answered, "I killed the ———." They asked him why he had done it and he explained that he had asked him to carry the bucket of water and the boy had refused to do so.

About a year after killing Osgood, Buck Harris got into trouble with a gambler over a game of cards. He called the gambler a foul name and reached for his pistol, but the gambler was too quick for him. He shot Harris in the mouth, killing him instantly.

Rancho Del Toro — Out near the Rio Grande was a ranch, which for convenience I shall call Del Toro. It was situated in a valley and surrounded by high hills, becoming a rendezvous for all the outlaws in this particular section. We heard several times of men that we wanted being there, but could not find them when we arrived.

The second lieutenant and I laid a plot to catch some of them. We rode into the ranch one day and inquired for persons for whom we gave fictitious names. They stated, of course, that they did not know these people. We bought some things at their store and went into camp near a well about a hundred yards from them. Late in the evening, we returned to the store and asked the way to a ranch about twenty miles from there. We also asked the storekeeper to give us a guide, which he did. When dusk came, we started in the direction of the ranch.

After we had traveled about four miles, the lieutenant halted us, telling us to take the bridles off the horses and lie down and hold them by their ropes so they could graze. We tied the guide to a tree until we were ready to start. Near daybreak we began moving back toward Del Toro where we arrived just before dawn.

The lieutenant gave orders for the company to form a circle around the ranch, behind the hills, telling us that when we heard him shoot, one man on each of the four sides of the ranch was to fire an answering shot. As the shots were fired, the whole command was to start in a fast run and close in on the ranch.

Until the time the shots were fired, the Mexicans at the ranch had suspected nothing, but when they saw men coming down the hills, bedlam broke loose. Some tried to run past the horsemen to get into the brush but were compelled to turn back. They began running from one house to another.

As soon as we had quieted them, the lieutenant and I went into the store and asked for one of the Mexicans for whom we were searching. The man replied that he was not there. With that, the lieutenant threw his gun down on him and told him to produce the man. The storekeeper turned to a peon who was standing by and told him to go after the man. The latter went into another room and brought him out.

After satisfying ourselves that no more of the men whom we wanted were there, we went into camp and began to prepare dinner. While we were so engaged, two Mexicans came riding up to the well where we were camped and stopped to talk to another Mexican. One of our own

Mexican scouts jumped to his feet and jerked one of the Mexicans off his horse. He was going to shoot him but we prevented this and asked him who the man was.

The scout said that he was one of the worst Mexicans in that country, that he had stabbed him (the scout) and left him for dead the year before, and that after stabbing him had stolen his horse and ravished his wife. He asked us to deputize him and two other Mexicans to take the prisoners to headquarters. We did this. We had to go to another ranch 30 miles from there on other business. When we arrived at headquarters, we found that the scouts with the prisoners had not arrived. The scouts came in later and reported that the other Mexicans had attacked them and the prisoners had been killed.

The Reappearance of Sam — Some time after our trip to Lagarto, Sam, the American we knew from Concepcion, disappeared but now he turned up again and began to get friendly with all the boys, and especially with the captain. He told some of the boys confidentially that he had discovered that they were soon to be disbanded and that when that happened, he would lead us to a place where more than a million dollars was concealed in a vault where it would be as easy to secure as taking candy from a child. He said it was on the opposite bank of the Rio Grande and that we could cross over and get it and be back in an hour. He explained that he wanted to hold us together after we were disbanded and that we would start at once. Some of the boys placed confidence in him and others did not.

In a few weeks we were ordered to disband[51] but scarcely half of the company would go (to cross the Rio Grande to

---

[51] Because of reported atrocities and incidents of ruthless behavior against Mexican-American citizens, the adjutant general of Texas, William Steele, disbanded Warren Wallace's Ranger company in

rob the vault). Theodore Priour[52] and I went into Bee and other counties trying to recruit men (for the venture). We established different points between Corpus Christi and the Rio Grande at which to hold our men until the final start. One rendezvous was on the Nueces River and another at the Los Olmos Ranch.[53]

John Priour,[54] Frank Bogus, Steve Burleson and one other were stationed at Los Olmos; the men enlisted by Theodore Priour and I were stationed on the Nueces River to wait until we came. When Priour and I could get no more men we went to the rendezvous on the Nueces and found it vacant.

We started for Los Olmos, but before we arrived there we heard that the boys had had a fight with some raiders and were supposed to have gone home to Corpus Christi. We rested for a few days and started for Corpus Christi.

One evening John Priour and a couple of the boys blew in. Priour said that some Mexicans attacked the store at Los Olmos, not knowing that the boys were there, as they were camped behind a horse pen. When they opened fire on the Mexicans, the Mexicans ran and the boys concluded that

---

September 1874. Steele conceded that Wallace's company had acted like "an armed mob." Neal Coldwell was appointed to take Wallace's place. From "Lone Star Justice" by Robert M. Utley. The Nueces Valley newspaper at Corpus Christi noted, "We have a report that Capt. Wallace caught several Mexicans at Concepcion and shot some and hanged others without so much as saying 'by your leave.' "

[52] Theodore Priour, from a well-known Corpus Christi family, later became a rancher.

[53] The Los Olmos Ranch was in what is now northern Brooks County.

[54] John M. Priour, brother of Theodore, later became well-known as a naturalist. He once said of the six years he spent as a "volunteer Ranger" that "our pistols were the law, judge and jury." From the "Pathfinders of Texas" by Mrs. Frank DeGarmo.

they would go on to Guerrero[55] and see if any of us had arrived.

John Priour and Frank Bogus[56] crossed the river, leaving two men in camp on the U.S. side. As soon as they stepped ashore, they were arrested by the Mexican guards and taken before the alcalde (or mayor), who grinned and asked them where the rest of the boys were. Priour told them that the other two were on the other side.

They were turned over to a file of soldiers, four of whom took Bogus with them to point out their camp. That evening Priour was summoned again before the alcalde. He told Priour that Sam, the man who had advised us in the scheme, had told him about our expected raid and that there was a reward of $1,000 out for me and Ferguson, which he would consider sufficient payment for betraying our party.

He showed Priour around the city and the garrison. There were about 900 troops in the place and all the flat-roofed houses were bristling with cannon. We would have been annihilated before we could have gotten into the town. After satisfying himself that there were no more of us, the alcalde permitted us to take our leave.

Something must have happened to Sam. He failed to report to his Mexican friends or to us. However, may the Rio Grande sing his lullaby.

To people not acquainted with conditions and customs at that time, our frustrated plan might have been classified as an attempt at robbery, but there was a more respectful name for it. It was called filibustering and it must be borne in mind that the Mexicans generally made about six raids to

---

[55] Guerrero, Coahuila, 35 miles downriver from Eagle Pass and Piedras Negras.

[56] Frank Boggus. He later rode on the posse with Henry Scott in search of the murderers of Thad Swift and his wife. From "A Vaquero of the Brush Country" by John D. Young and J. Frank Dobie.

one made by Americans. In other words, you scratch my back and I'll scratch yours.

Murder of Mr. Hatch — On the 7th of June, 1872, Mr. George Hatch, an old and respected citizen, was shot to death in his buggy on the north side of the reef.[57] This happened in full view of the town. Mr. Hatch was an early settler who owned a splendid vineyard at Ingleside. His habit of making a weekly trip to Corpus Christi for mail and supplies was undoubtedly known to his assassins, who laid in wait and shot him on one of these occasions.

The old man fell across the dashboard of his buggy. He was in a kneeling position. The murderers cut out his pockets and robbed him, after which they took his horses and fled. Outside of five or six persons, no one knows whether they were caught or not.

Mr. Hatch was 83 years of age when he was murdered. Several years after his death, we captured some Mexican murderers and got a confession from them in which they named the two men who murdered Mr. Hatch. Every time we captured a Mexican we listened to his confession and placed the names he gave us in our plug hats for future reference. But instead of giving them absolution for their sins, we transferred that part of the matter to the Deity and left them to settle it with Him, as we claimed no jurisdiction over such matters.

It is amusing to hear people say that the murderers of so-and-so in those days were never caught. Well, ignorance is bliss.

---

[57] The reef across Nueces Bay was used as an underwater passageway between Corpus Christi and Portland.

96

Burning of Noakes' Store by Mexican Raiders April 26, 1875

CHAPTER TEN

THE MEXICAN RAID[58]

The Warning — On the morning of the 26th of March 1875, my brother Matt and I, together with Pat[59] and George Dunn, rode to town to look after some business. We had just returned home and unsaddled our horses when one of the Stevens boys[60] from Tule Lake came in a run and handed us a note. The note was from John Dunn[61] telling us that the Mexicans were robbing the Page house[62] at Tule Lake. He told us to hurry up and come and that he would join us as we passed his house. He also told us to send Stevens to town as quickly as possible, as he was also sending a letter to John McClane, the sheriff, telling him to send men to help as there would be only four of us against about seventy Mexicans.

---

[58] This is variously called the Nuecestown Raid, where many of the events occurred, or the Noakes Raid, because Thomas J. Noakes' store was burned, or the Corpus Christi Raid, since that town was believed to have been the original objective of the raiders.

[59] Pat F. Dunn was later known as the Duke of Padre Island.

[60] Willie Stevens, the son of a neighbor to the Dunns.

[61] The other John Dunn was the writer's cousin.

[62] Sydney Page, a cattle drover, had a large family at his ranch and homestead on Tule Lake.

After starting Stevens to town, we saddled our horses and started in a gallop for Tule Lake.[63] As we passed John Dunn's place, he joined us and we went on, feeling that it would be but a few moments until a company with rifles headed by the sheriff would be with us.

When we arrived at Page's, we found no one there but two girls, one of them being a Miss Louisa Rains, a sister of Mrs. Charles Golihar of Sunshine, Texas, and a daughter of Mr. Page. They told us that when the raiders had taken everything they wanted, they took all the men on the place prisoners and started toward the Juan Saenz ranch.[64] At that time the ranch was considerably larger than it is now. So we started out after the Mexicans.

When we arrived there, we found the raiders busy rounding up the stock and the prisoners. They had the latter lined up against George Frank's store. We took a position about a thousand or eight hundred yards from them, where we could see everything that took place and also watch the road. It had now been three hours since we had sent word to town and we had received no aid as yet. John Dunn told us if we would keep watch he would go to town and see if he could raise a few men.

Mr. Borden Is Taken Prisoner — John Dunn took a shortcut and started off at a gallop. Shortly after he left, Sidney Borden, a merchant and justice of the peace at Sharpsburg, came driving up in his buggy. We stopped him, showed him the Mexicans, told him what they were doing and advised him to turn back. He stated that he did not think they would molest him and drove on. We saw

---

[63] Tule Lake, a salt lake, is located west of Corpus Christi along UpRiver Road.

[64] Juan Saenz was a community nine miles west of Corpus Christi. The principal establishment was George Frank's store.

three Mexicans ride out to where he was approaching and escort him over to where the prisoners were. It seemed that there were more people traveling the road that day than we had ever seen in a day before.[65]

Capture of Mike Dunn — Shortly after Borden's capture, Mike Dunn, a brother of John Dunn, drove up in a buggy right into the midst of the Mexicans. The leader rode out and stopped him, taking a Sharp's carbine that Mike had in the buggy and told him to hand over his ammunition. He had only four or five cartridges in his pocket, which he gave them. The leader told Mike to tell his wife, who was with him, not to be uneasy, that she would not be harmed.

A Prisoner Is Killed — While rounding up the prisoners, the Mexicans drove a bunch of other Mexicans out of a jacal and started them to where the other prisoners were under guard. While on the way, one of the new prisoners wheeled around and started to run back toward the jacal. One of the raiders put his Winchester to the man's head and blew his brains out. Later we learned that the unfortunate man was an idiot.

The Star Rifles Refuse to Help — It was now beginning to grow late, and we feared that perhaps John Dunn must have been waylaid, as it did not seem reasonable that people would act in that manner, refusing to send help. There was a company of Star Rifles fully equipped in Corpus and not one of them left town that day.[66]

---

[65] It was Good Friday and many were on their way to Corpus Christi to attend church services.

[66] Dunn apparently was wrong about the Star Rifles. Eli T. Merriman and E. H. Caldwell said the organization was not in existence at the

We Pursue the Ladies — When the raiders were ready to leave the Juan Saenz ranch, they rounded up all the men prisoners and drove them ahead, going straight up the old Nuecestown road. They left the women behind at the ranch.

As soon as they moved out, we moved in. Some of the women saw us advancing and thought we were more Mexicans, so a number of them ran into the chaparral. We caught them and brought them back to the ranch. We also caught some horses that the raiders had left and started the ladies for town, hitching the horses to the buggies that the raiders had captured. Some of the ladies were not found for a couple of days, being finally located by Charlie McKenzie and his brother.[67]

Meanwhile, the raiders were driving the prisoners ahead of them in a long trot, beating them with quirts and ropes and punching them with their guns and pistols. Just as we were leaving the ranch on their trail, we met a stockman by the name of Bass Burris (a relative of Martin Culver). With him was Clem Vetters, now janitor of the high school, and three Mexicans. All the Mexicans were unarmed. We took to the trail again, still expecting help from town. When we caught up with the raiders, we were at Noake's[68] store at Nuecestown. It was nearly sundown, but there was still no help from Corpus.

The raiders were not seen from the store until they had the place surrounded. Most of them dismounted. Mr. Noakes was in a backroom and, hearing a noise in front, he rushed out. Just as he reached the front door, a Mexican

---

time of the raid, that it was formed later, as a consequence of the raid. From "Recollections of Other Days."

[67] They were Mrs. E. D. Sidbury, the wife of a Corpus Christi lumber dealer, and her daughter, Mrs. R. Savage, and Miss Laura Allen.

[68] Thomas J. Noakes, who came to Corpus Christi from England and settled at Nuecestown.

came rushing in with a cocked Winchester in his hand. Noakes fired at him and shot him through the breast. With that, Noakes dropped through a trap door in the floor and into some trenches underground. Another man by the name of Smith,[69] who happened to be there, followed Noakes into the trench.

The Mexicans entered the store and after piling up outside all that they wanted to confiscate, they set fire to the building, hoping to burn Noakes out. Every time they would get the fire started, Mrs. Noakes would pour water on it. So at last two of them caught her and held her until the fire got a good start.

Shooting of Smith — In the meantime, Mr. Noakes held the trench. But, finally, the smoke and heat got so bad that Smith crawled out and made a run for the river. Some of the raiders followed him and shot him down. He fell on his face and they put their carbines to his back and shot him four times, all the balls coming out of his breast. Two years ago I heard from him and he was still alive and hearty.[70]

The Raiders Leave the Store — As the raiders did not know that Noakes had another man with him, they thought that they had killed Noakes when they got Smith, and were, therefore, satisfied. They took the wounded Mexican Noakes had shot and put him in a wagon, also piling in the goods they had stolen from the store. They also put in several prisoners, among them Billy McKenzie, a brother of Charles McKenzie of Nuecestown, and Judge Ball[71] of

---

[69] John "Windy" or "Lying" Smith.

[70] Smith said later, "If ever another man takes a shot to kill me, he had better aim at my heels, 'cause I can sure run under pressure."

[71] W. A. Ball, a stockraiser and justice of the peace at Nuecestown.

Nuecestown. They started in a southwest direction, leaving the main road. The sun was almost setting.

John Dunn Returns — Just at that time John Dunn returned from town. He had only four men with him, my brother James, Pat Whalen, a man from Duval County named Swank and Wash Mussett.[72] John informed us that the people of Corpus would not send anyone because they claimed they needed the men there. We concluded that we would not let the Mexicans go without giving them a slight reception.

The Reception Committee Acts — The raiders had taken a trail into the chaparral. One of the boys informed us that a short distance away the trail forked in opposite directions and that it would be a good idea for two men with good horses to go ahead of the rest and see which trail they were taking. John Dunn and Swank volunteered to go. A few hundred yards ahead we met John Dunn coming back alone. We asked him where Swank was and he said he did not know as he had gone in the opposite direction and he had not seen him since. He told us that the raiders were congregated around the wagon in a small glade in the mesquite.

The raiders were continually firing off their arms, so it was not hard to trail them. When we came upon them in the glade, they were all concentrated around the wagon that held the prisoners, the wounded Mexican Noakes had shot, and the loot from the stores.

We were within a hundred yards of them before they saw us. When we started to charge them, the man Burris told his

---

[72] George Swank, a carpenter from Corpus Christi, and Washington ("Wash") Mussett.

three unarmed Mexicans to line up alongside of him, threatening to shoot them if they turned back, but just as soon as we started after the raiders two of them wheeled their horses and broke away through space.

The bullets were singing lullabies all around us. Among them we could recognize the sound of Mike Dunn's old sharpshooter of which he had been relieved at Juan Saenz. The lead in the end of the cartridges had been split down to the brass shell and their scream was like the wail of a lost soul.

Before we reached the raiders, they broke and scattered like a covey of quail. At the same time, the prisoners jumped out of the back end of the wagon and scattered into the brush. It was dusk and soon they were out of sight and we were out of ammunition. Some of us had two or three cartridges, and the most any of us had was five.

We returned to W. M. McGregor's store at Nuecestown, but could get nothing but .44 rim-fire cartridges which would fit the Winchesters and .44 Colts, but three of us were armed with .50 caliber sharpshooters.[73] When we arrived at the store, there were a number of men assembled there.

We tried to get them to come with us to Banquete, where there were several ranches at which we could probably secure help, but they positively refused to go with us to overtake the raiders. That is, they all refused except one man, a Mr. Hunter.[74] The others stated that it would be suicide to think of it, believing that we would be waylaid and murdered.

---

[73] Dunn was probably referring to the popular .50 caliber Sharps Carbine.

[74] James M. Hunter, a Confederate veteran, owned a livery stable in Corpus Christi.

The names of the men that took part in the fight with the raiders were Matt Dunn, John Dunn, Pat Dunn, James Dunn, Bass Burris, Clem Vetters, George Dunn, Wash Mussett, Jesus Seguira, Pat Whalen and I. There was also George Swank who was killed.

We Follow the Raiders —We started with the one recruit for Banquete. We had had no dinner and no supper and were hungry when we arrived at daybreak next morning. However, Mr. T. Hines Clark, a cattle rancher, gave us a fine breakfast.

Had the raiders known how we were fixed in regard to ammunition they could have turned on us and cleaned us up in a very few minutes. One of the Mexicans that was with Burris stayed right with us during the whole time of the shooting. His name was Jesus Seguira. I shall have occasion to mention him in a later article. He was as brave as they make them. Years before he had been one of Cortina's lieutenants during that celebrated bandit's raids on the Texas border and he knew Mexican tactics to a finish. He had but one fault and that was drunkenness. When he was drunk he was very dangerous.

Long since, some people circulated the report that the Mexican raiders insulted the women at Nuecestown. It is a false report. The raiders must be given credit for treating the women courteously and not molesting them in any manner.

A Battle with Mexican Raiders at old Nuecestown, April 26, 1875

CHAPTER ELEVEN

TRIP TO THE SAND

The First Trip — My brother Matt, George Dunn and myself joined Capt. T. Hines Clark's company[75] and started for the Sand, or lower country, where there were a large number of Mexican ranches, among them La Travisada, La Mesa, La Prieta, El Mesquite, and others I cannot now recall.

These ranches harbored large groups of men whose sole occupation was killing cattle belonging to American stock men. They sold the hides to merchants who had small stores at some of the ranches. At most of the ranches were large buildings packed full of dried hides, in addition to pits dug in the sand that were also filled with dry hides.

At the Mesquite Ranch, a man named Blaine had a store and purchased hides from the Mexicans. I will have occasion to mention him later.

When we reached the Sand, we found the whole country covered with the carcasses of cattle that had been killed for their hides. I will not state if we captured any of the raiders in our travels, because if we did, and they sent any message back, I have forgotten it. We remained only a short time and then returned. The country referred to as the Sand was

---

[75] They were called "minutemen," vigilante volunteers ready to ride at a moment's notice. Clark's company was described as "revengeful law bringers" in "A Vaquero of the Brush Country."

so named on account of the numerous sand dunes in that section.

Our Second Trip — After being home a few days, we heard that the Mexicans were gathering in force and we hurried back with the intention of meeting them. When we arrived at the ranches, we found them deserted. But when we came to the Mesquite Ranch, we were surprised to find the man Blaine standing in the door of his store with two pistols around his waist. As there was no one in particular in charge of our expedition at the time, we had no understanding as to what disposal to make of Blaine. In fact, we did not expect to find him there.

So we rode up to the porch and stopped there on our horses, no one saying a word. Blaine said, "Is that the crowd from the river?"

Just as he spoke, a Mexican came walking up the steps. When he got to the door where Blaine stood, one of the boys told him to halt. With that, he grabbed for one of his pistols and was instantly riddled (with bullets) by someone. Blaine slammed the door shut, after firing one of his pistols at us. As he did this, we fired a volley into the door. The firing became general from inside and out.

The shooting had been going on for about fifteen minutes when we saw a white flag sticking up on top of a small lookout on the building. We stopped shooting and Blaine stuck his head out and asked us what we wanted of him. One of the men told him we wanted the keys to the store, that we wished to search for stolen hides. He asked us to give him fifteen minutes, which we agreed to do.

When the time was up, Blaine was notified but would make no answer. The shooting commenced again. There were three in our crowd who never fired a shot, myself, my brother Matt, and George Dunn. We had known Blaine for a long time and he had done favors for us, so we could not harm him. We tried to persuade the boys to let him go but they seemed determined to get him.

Someone suggested setting fire to the house, but no one seemed anxious to undertake the job. We had a Mexican with us, whom we had picked up at King Ranch on our way down. His name was Luis Robelos. When Luis saw that no one was going to volunteer to fire the house, he went to a nearby jacal and pulled a lot of straw out of the roof. He lit the straw and, mounting his horse, galloped to the building and threw the blazing straw on top of a shed that joined the main building. It burned slowly for a few minutes and then the roof caught fire.

Blaine, observing this, burst a hole through the roof and began throwing water on the fire. We told the boys that if they shot at him, we would quit and go home. We told them that Blaine would never buy any more hides and that all he wanted was to escape. They finally agreed with us and we left him alone in his glory.

We Make a Third Trip — Several days after the above incident we had occasion to visit the place again. We found it vacated and the building looked as if it had been riddled by machine guns. A number of our boys were armed with .50 caliber carbines. They had a habit of splitting the lead ball down to the edge of the brass shell so that when the guns were fired off they would let out a terrible piercing scream and would tear a hole that a rat could run into.

A Place of Desolation — The empty store was a mess. There were shoes with the heels torn off by bullets and hats with three or four bullets in them. An awful stench came from the canned goods where the cans had been perforated by bullets.

There was one big building made of live oak posts put down in the ground with the spaces between them daubed up with mud and moss. This building had port holes through which one could shoot on either side. We stopped at this place, intending to remain there for the night, it now being late in the evening. Some of the boys had already unsaddled their horses, among them my brother Matt. There were large live oak trees all around the house and Matt was tying his horse to one of them when he heard stock running.

An Exciting Moment — Matt looked up and saw two Mexicans with a bunch of horses. They were driving the animals to a pen about fifty yards away. Matt dodged behind a tree and waited until they had penned the horses and closed the gate. Just as they were ready to mount their horses, he threw down on them and told them to halt. Instead of doing this, they jumped into their saddles, struck a gallop and began firing as they ran.

Three of our boys (one of them being the Mexican, Jesus Seguira, who had been with us at Nuecestown) followed them. One of the Mexican's horses that had been wounded in the shooting at the pen could not keep up with the others, so his owner made for a vacant camp in the live oaks. There he jumped from his horse and ran under a wagon where he was captured. The other Mexican got away into the thick oak shrubbery.

We Are Attacked — We found a beef dressed and hanging up in the camp and also two wagons loaded with corn and other things. We asked the prisoner whose camp it was and where its occupants were, but all he would do was grin and say, "You will find out."

A few moments after he had been brought into camp, we heard a bugle sound in a southeasterly direction. It was answered from the opposite direction. Now we knew what the vacant camp meant.

One of the boys, named Singleton, climbed to the top of the highest jacal and called out to us saying, "They are coming from the four quarters of the earth, boys. Clouds of sand everywhere you look."

At the same time, there were cow horns and bugles sounding all around and in a few minutes they had the camp surrounded, forming a circle about a hundred yards from us. There must have been at least a hundred of them, while there were only ten of us.

It was almost sunset. There was considerable excitement among us. Some of us wanted to stay and fight and others argued that if we did, the Mexicans would get behind the oaks and set fire to the straw-covered houses and shoot us as we came out. This we knew to be true.

Seguira Is Put in Command — The Mexican, Jesus Seguira, had at one time been a lieutenant in Cortina's[76] forces and understood Mexican tactics. So we instructed him to take charge and told him we would obey his orders. He formed us in line, single file, putting the prisoner in the rear with a man behind him with orders to shoot him if the Mexicans fired on us.

As we lined up, he told us to have our guns cocked with the butts resting on our hips and to ride just as slowly as our horses could walk, not letting a single horse stumble, as

---

[76] Gen. Juan Nepomuceno (Cheno) Cortina commanded border raiders that preyed on South Texas ranches. "Rip" Ford said he was fearless and cunning but lacked a well-defined idea of property rights. From "Rip Ford's Texas" by Stephen B. Oates and "Lone Star" by T. R. Fehrenbach.

the Mexicans might think we were going to run. He asked one of the boys to ride over to the head man and ask him the direction to a certain place.

We picked out the man we thought to be the captain, as he was riding the finest horse and giving orders. When our man got within fifty yards of him, he motioned him to fall back, which he did. We all moved on to where the captain was and when we got within fifty yards of him, he made a motion to his men and they opened a space for us to pass through. We could hardly believe that we were going to get away that easily.

Seguira Saves the Day — Jesus rode along the line talking to us, fully believing they would yet turn on us. Still, he would not allow us to change our pace or let a single horse trot. "If we trot," he said, "they will get suspicious and think we are going to make a break."

The sun was only a few minutes high when we passed through their lines. After we were about a hundred yards away, they began to move in the direction of the ranch. Jesus sent out two men on each side of our column and one to stay some distance behind us, to keep watch so that they would not be able to slip up on us. As soon as it began to get dark, he told us to strike a trot and later ordered us to gallop. We kept on galloping until we reached Bovido Creek[77] to which Jesus thought the Mexicans might beat us and hide in the big gullies on each side of the road at the crossing. Our prisoner is still somewhere in that creek, as he fell off his horse and Jesus shot him, thinking he was an alligator. At this place we rested for a day or so and went back again.

---

[77] The creek, also known as Bobedo, empties into Baffin Bay. The word came from the Rincon de la Boveda grant.

We Return — We scouted all over the same ground and could not find a soul. Every one of the ranches was deserted. Some pyromaniac must have been following us, for every time we passed through a ranch it mysteriously caught on fire.[78]

A Pitiful Sight — At one of the ranches we found an old Mexican woman who looked as if she might have passed the century mark. She was kneeling beside a mound of earth with a cross on it about four feet high and was muttering and praying without seeming in the least alarmed. The boys crowded around her and she told them that her son was buried there, that he had been murdered by some of the Mexicans on the ranch. She implored us to kill every one of them that we could find, saying that they were all thieves and murderers. They had left the unfortunate creature without any water and she was nearly dead with thirst. We went into the jacals and collected all the food we could find and took the well bucket and filled it with water. We watched her jacal until the others had finished burning and moved on.

We Arrive at King Ranch — The next morning we reached King Ranch just as day was breaking. It had been blowing a hard south wind during the early part of the night and this had carried the smoke from the burning ranches all the way to Santa Gertrudis.

---

[78] The burned ranches led Nueces County Sheriff John McClane to send a telegram to the adjutant general, William Steele: "Is Capt. McNelly coming. We are in trouble. Five ranches burned by disguised men near La Parra last week. Answer." From "Lone Star" by T. R. Fehrenbach, "The Men Who Wear the Star" by Charles M. Robinson III, and "The Texas Rangers" by Walter Prescott Webb.

When we got close to the ranch, we saw someone walking back and forth in front of it and when we got closer we saw that it was Captain King. "What is the matter boys," he greeted us; "has a volcano broken loose?" We explained the situation, telling him how all the houses had caught fire and burned up, except the buildings that had hides in them, and he said to us, "There are plenty of teams and wagons here, hitch them up, go and get the hides, sell them and keep the money." We told him we did not care to fool with them, so he said, "Well, go back and burn them." This we did.

Jesus Gets Drunk — There being no more ranches in that section, we started homeward. As we came into an open space between two bunches of timber, we saw a large body of horsemen coming out of the timber in front of us. We halted a moment and watched them. They formed a line on the prairie facing us.

As we were just in the edge of the timber, we had the advantage of them. We noticed a man leaving the line and coming toward us with a white flag. He rode up and asked who was in command and our captain was pointed out to him. He informed our captain that he had orders for us to disband, explaining that he had been sent there to take charge of that territory and introducing himself as Captain McNelly. Our captain[79] told him that this was agreeable as we were on our way home.

We went into camp that night at the Bovido Ranch, where McNelly's company also camped. The night before we had camped near this same ranch and Jesus Seguira, finding some mescal, had gotten gloriously drunk. He stayed on at the ranch after we had gone, and we did not know where he

---

[79] T. Hines Clark, a cattle rancher and vigilante leader.

was. The next morning after breakfast we started out, leaving the cook to hitch up and follow us. When we got into McNelly's camp, we were surprised to find the cook shot in the ankle and Jesus a prisoner.

It seems that the cook had let one of the wagon horses get away from him and was chasing him on the prairie. Jesus, meanwhile, had come into camp and found it deserted. He saw the cook on the prairie and gave chase to him, thinking he was trying to desert. He first fired a shot over the cook's head in an attempt to halt him. The cook fired back at Jesus. Jesus alighted from his horse, and resting his Winchester across his saddle, fired at the cook, shooting him in the ankle and knocking him down.

Jesus Escapes — When Jesus saw us coming back with McNelly's men, he cried like a baby, thinking we were prisoners like himself. McNelly tried to get us to join his company but we refused.[80] He asked Captain Clark to detail three men to take Jesus to Corpus Christi and turn him over to the sheriff. Captain Clark detailed George Dunn, my brother Matt, and me.

When we got within four miles of town, Jesus wheeled his horse and ran away from us. He was riding a fine gray stallion, and the night being dark, he was soon lost in the

---

[80] Various accounts of Leander McNelly's exploits tell a different story. McNelly ordered Clark to disband and disarm his men, or that he, McNelly, would do it for him. From "The Men Who Wear the Star" by Charles M. Robinson III. When Clark's men offered to surrender their weapons to McNelly, he said later, this was the moment when he and the Texas Rangers officially became the law in South Texas. From "Leander McNelly: Texas Ranger" by Bob Scott. In "Taming the Nueces Strip," George Durham said Martin Culver, the cattleman, was also part of the vigilante band.

chaparral. We fired a farewell salute to him and went and reported to the sheriff.

A Last Encounter — About four months after that, we were at San Patricio attending court and were camped a few hundred yards from Captain Hall's company, which was once McNelly's company, when who should walk out of their camp and into ours but Jesus Seguira. He told us that he was Captain Hall's servant and that there were two of the men in the company that had belonged to McNelly's company and had helped to arrest him at the time he shot our cook, but that they had never recognized him. This was the last time I ever saw Jesus Seguira. No braver man ever lived. In the fight at Nuecestown he stayed right with us during the whole encounter, although he did not have so much as a pocket knife.

There is no doubt, whatever, that if it had not been for him, when we were surrounded by the Mexicans at Mesquite Ranch, that we would have been annihilated, as there were but ten of us and at least a hundred of them.

Courageous Mexicans — It is a mistaken idea, sometimes prevalent, to believe that all Mexicans are cowards. There were two Mexicans with us and they would go into places that few white men would dare to go.

A Strange Kind of Gratitude — After we had chased the bandits across the Rio Grande and made the country safe for Americans, we had to undergo another system of persecution from the home people whom we had helped to defend. We were indicted for killing Mexicans who never existed.[81] This made us desperate after a manner and caused us to get into other trouble. We were placed under the heaviest bonds, amounting to $67,000. I had to attend court in three different counties. It is all over now and I have won out and have no apologies to offer. I merely took St. Paul's advice and while in Rome did as the Romans did.[82]

---

[81] Dunn and other Rangers were tried for murder and robbery involving offenses committed as members of Warren Wallace's Ranger company, which was disbanded because of several atrocities and extra-judicial murders. Dunn and others were acquitted but the details of that trial were lost when the San Patricio County Courthouse, then at the village of San Patricio, burned in 1889. In "Lone Star Justice," Robert Utley wrote that Warren Wallace's company, part of the Frontier Battalion, "behaved so ruthlessly against Mexican residents of Texas that an officer and some men wound up in court charged with murder and robbery."

[82] The minute companies around Corpus Christi (one of which Dunn belonged to) staged counter-raids, not across the border, but against suspected ethnic allies of the bandits. On one of these excursions, 11 men were executed. From "Lone Star" by T. R. Fehrenbach.

CHAPTER TWELVE

A HOT TIME IN OLD SAN PAT

We Go to the Circus —After the Mexican raid, after we had made the country safe for Americans, and after we had been indicted for the disappearance of every Mexican who did not respond when his mama called, and after it was proven that we could not get a fair and impartial trial in Corpus Christi, we secured a change of venue to San Patricio County.

At that time San Patricio was the county seat and was a thriving village consisting of about four stores, a Catholic church, a convent, two boarding houses and plenty of whiskey.

Mrs. Ryan ran the principal boarding house and we made our headquarters there. Cherokee Brown ran the other boarding house.[83] San Pat at that time was a very lively place.

Mrs. Ryan's hotel was a large two-story frame building. The upstairs was one solid room without any ceiling and but one bedstead that stood in the middle of the room. The rest of the room was lined with cots.

---

[83] Another boarding house during this period was run by Eliza Sullivan, which was directly across from the courthouse. From "The Forgotten Colony: San Patricio de Hibernia" by Rachel Bluntzer Hebert.

On the first day of our arrival, a circus came to the place. Mr. Hubert Timon was sheriff at that time. Just at dark he came to us and said, "Buckle on your pistols, boys, I am going to deputize all of you so you will be admitted to the circus free." We thanked him and did as he said.

When about half of us were inside, the manager yelled out, "Are all the men in this and adjoining counties deputies?" The sheriff told him to keep his shirt on, that a third of them were not there yet and to reserve seats for them. Someone told the manager to go and butt his head against a tent pole, and he quieted down.

The Dance at McCloskey Hall — The next night there was a dance at McCloskey Hall, an entertainment gotten up for the benefit of the church. Again the sheriff came to the door where we were watching the dancing and told us to put on our guns and go inside. We thanked him and told him we had a very good view from where we were.

It was the first time that we had ever seen people dancing with pistols and knives on them and it was amusing in the extreme. There was quite a variety of pistols displayed. Those who were wealthy had beautiful pearl- and ivory-handled ones nicely inlaid with gold and silver. Others were so rusty that it would have seemed like suicide to cock one of them. At times when a fellow would give his girl a hard swing, the handle of his pistol would sometimes strike the handle of the pistol belonging to the man dancing nearest him. If it got a good hard jolt, he would stop dancing and pull the weapon out and examine it, to see if it had been damaged, while the dancers stood spellbound awaiting the verdict. After cocking it a time or two and finding it was OK, they would proceed with the dance.

The only incident that tended to mar the harmony of the proceedings was caused by a young man who had been appointed to collect the funds. About an hour before daylight he went to a gambling table and lost all he had collected. However, be it said to the credit of the gamblers who won it, that as soon as they found out that the money belonged to the church they returned every cent of it. Their names are worth mentioning. One was Mr. Stapleton and the other Mr. Van Doren.

The McConel Incident — Among those who came to San Patricio to attend court[84] was an attorney named McConel.[85] The Garner brothers employed him to defend them in a case that they had pending. McConel was what might be called a scientific booze-fighter, and he proceeded at once to defend his title.

About the first place he went to was a saloon where he called for some "furius et aqua fortis" and told the bar man to sweeten it with brimstone, skim it with a cyclone and stir it with a lightning-rod. After he had imbibed about four drinks, two Mexicans were employed to carry the attorney back to Mrs. Ryan's boarding house. They took him upstairs and placed him in the one large bed that the room boasted.

About twelve o'clock, one of the Garner brothers came and asked me to go upstairs with him. He wanted to find out if his lawyer was going to be in a fit condition to attend to his case, should it be called for trial the following day.

When we arrived upstairs, we found him sprawled out on the bed with all his clothes off except a very short shirt and the bed filled with cakes of soap, old shoes, etc., and

---

[84] The courthouse at San Patricio was a new structure built by Viggo Kohler in 1872. It burned in 1889 and the county seat was moved to Sinton. From the "History of San Patricio County" by Keith Guthrie.

[85] He was probably referring to a Corpus Christi attorney, James D. McConnell.

someone had even thrown a pitcher of water on him. We tried to awaken him with negligible results.

I proposed to Garner that I go down in the lot and swipe Mrs. Ryan's clothes line and that we tie it around one of his ankles and shove the other end of the rope over one of the rafters and then taking that same end, go about half way down the stairs and pull slowly on the rope until we had his leg straight and then tie it to one of the banisters and go down and mix with the crowd until the exposition started.

After carrying out our plan to the letter, we did not have long to wait. When he hit the floor, it sounded like a cotton bale had struck it, jarring the whole house. We heard fearful screams and pleas to "Take the alligator out of my bed! It is eating my leg off!" There must have been about forty people in the house at the time and they all rushed upstairs with their pistols in their hands, not knowing what had happened. Mrs. Ryan brought up the rear, armed with a bed slat, and when she got there one of the men threw a quilt over the victim and began cutting the rope from his ankles. Mrs. Ryan made a few clips at him, but the boys warded off the blows. He was advised not to go to town any more, since some people were watching for him and if they caught him, they were going to throw him in the river to drown. He was very quiet that night and next morning he bade farewell to San Pat.

Old Uncle Billy — Late next day an ambulance[86] with two fine horses driven by a Mexican drove up to the Ryan House. In the ambulance was a ranchman who for convenience I shall call Uncle Billy. He ordered his driver to drive into the horse lot and unhitch the horses while he

---

[86] "Ambulance" then referred to a two-wheeled light spring carriage.

went uptown to hunt some tarantula juice. When he returned he was full to the neck.

He wanted Mrs. Ryan to let him sleep in the room downstairs where the judge and the attorneys were sleeping, but she positively refused to do so. It was then night and she told him to go upstairs and get himself a cot. When I saw him start, I hurried and got ahead of him and pushing my cot next to the wall, filled it with all kinds of plunder, broken washstands, chairs, and anything I could find. When he arrived and found but the one vacant cot, he began taking the things out of it and throwing them against the floor which awoke those who were asleep in the other cots. They immediately opened a barrage of soap from the washstands followed by chairs, boots and anything they could put their hands on.

When the people below heard the noise, they made a rush upstairs, Mrs. Ryan with her bed slat bringing up the rear. When they arrived, Uncle Billy was standing in the middle of the floor, with the cot spread out, using it as a shield to ward off the missiles the boarders were firing at him. Mrs. Ryan made a clip at him with the bed slat and missed him. If she had hit him, he would doubtless have been minus an ear.

"What the divil is the matter with ye?" she asked him. He replied, "Do you think I could sleep on an alligator like that?" pointing to the cot. Some of the boys wanted to tie him up until daylight but he promised them that if they would forbear he would go and sleep somewhere else. They let him go and he went uptown, only to crawl upstairs again about an hour afterwards.

He went over in the corner right over the bed where the judge and the district attorney were asleep and lay there groaning and cursing everyone. Ever so often he would kick the floor with his heels. After a while, he got up and went out on the porch, facing the lot where his driver and horses were, and called out, "Jose! Jose![87] Bring up a bucket of water. My abdomen is on fire!" When the Mexican came with the water he lay down on his back and pulling up his shirt, made the man pour the water slowly on his stomach.

In a few moments, all was confusion. As the floor was not tongued or grooved, the water poured down into the beds below and there was wailing and gnashing of teeth. Some caught hold of him and were preparing to tie him up for the balance of the night but he pleaded so pitifully that they relented. It seemed to satisfy him that he had routed the judge and the district attorney out of their roost, and he did no more antics.

Next morning when he was getting ready to leave he called out, "Come on, boys, and kiss papa bye bye. We had a lot of fun but wait till next time. We will give the menfolks one hour to move the women and children out of town and then we will set fire to it." With this he entered his carriage and started for his ranch and we cheered him as long as he was in sight. Goodbye, Uncle Billy!

Another Knight of Fire and Brimstone — Attorney McManigle was another scientific booze-fighter who came to San Pat to attend court. On the second night after his arrival, he went up in the north of town to visit a friend. It was a common thing when the mosquitos were bad for the cattle to bed on the public road, which was also the main street.

It was early in the evening when McManigle started out and there were but few cattle on the street at the time. Mac and his friend finished a quart that his friend had in the

---

[87] In the original manuscript, Dunn spells Jose as Hosa.

house and about twelve o'clock Mac started home. By that time the road was covered with cattle. Mac got no more than ten feet from the house when he stumbled over a cow, which arose and tossed him on another cow, who in turn tossed him on another, etc., until finally he reached home. During the intervals that he was not on a cow's back he was in a pile of manure.

He stated that at one time he thought the road, street and cattle were going around in a circle. For a moment it looked as if the revolutions had stopped. He thought he detected a small vacant spot and made a jump for it, landing in a bunch of calves, who kicked him and cut him with their sharp hoofs, finally landing him in more manure.

He was the most comical sight that we had ever seen when he finally arrived. His hair, whiskers and clothes were matted with manure, and after we got through laughing at him, he wound up by putting a curse on San Pat. He said that he hoped it would be set afloat in an open boat and that the boat would be swallowed by a shark who would be swallowed by a whale, and the whale would be landed in the northeast corner of Hades, the door of which would be locked and the key lost. He wound up by saying, "I now christen that street Cow Chip Lane." The next morning he pulled his freight for Corpus Christi.

The Derringer Incident — Mrs. Ryan's dining table would seat at least thirty-five people. The food was put in dishes and passed up and down the table as people called for it. About the only fruit that we indulged in in those days was dried apples, which looked as if they had been smoked instead of merely dried.

On this particular day two small butter dishes of this delicacy were placed, one at each end of the table. Each dish contained about one teacup of the fruit. A rube who was sitting near the lower end of the table asked the man next to him what was in the dish. "Fruit," answered the person questioned. The rube grabbed the dish and emptied the contents in his plate and began working on them. He happened to spy the other dish at the far end of the table and cried out, "Pass the fruit." With that one of the boarders at the upper end of the table started it toward him. When it came to where Pat Dunn was sitting, he took the dish of fruit and setting it down, picked up an empty dish. At the same time he slipped his hand in the coat pocket of the man next to him and extracted a large derringer that he knew the man was carrying. Placing it in the empty dish, he started it down to the rube, who was so busy sopping out with a piece of bread the last drop of apple juice that he never noticed what had been going on until the man with the dish said, "Here is your fruit." The rube flew into a tantrum and got up and left, going to Cherokee Brown's. Thus Mrs. Ryan lost a boarder and thereafter he would not notice any of us when he met us on the street.

A San Pat Cocktail — Among the merchants in San Pat was a man whom we shall call the Proprietor. He owned a small grocery store and as an inducement to his customers kept a line of cocktails, gin and whiskey. While in his store one day one of the boys asked for a cocktail. He turned to his son, a small boy, and said, to him, "Son, go out in the yard and pull out that old red rooster's tail and bring it to me." He turned to the one who ordered the cocktail and said to him, "I'll wait on you, young man, when the boy comes back." But when the boy returned, he said to his father, "I can't catch him, pa." "That's all right, son," said the old man, "let him go."

We could see by the way that he looked at us that he thought we were poking fun at him but he was not quite sure. So to make matters more pleasant, one of the boys ordered a bottle of cocktail and invited him to drink with us. This he did and we parted good friends.

The next day the news was all over town and was causing a lot of mirth. In the evening one of the residents came to us and proposed that about twenty-five of us should go to the store in a body and let four or five of the strongest men place themselves near the proprietor, so that if he made a break when we ordered our cocktails, we could catch him and hold him until he quieted down.

This plan we carried out. On arrival, one of the boys cried out, "Give me a cocktail." The whole crowd chorused, "I will take the same." The Proprietor stood looking at us foolishly for a moment and said, "Boys, I appreciate your order but unfortunately I have but one rooster on the place and have not tails enough to go around. However, I am expecting a coop of chickens this evening and if there are enough roosters to go around, you shall have cocktails tonight." We emptied about four bottles of bitters and cocktails in which the man joined us and we parted good friends. As we were leaving, he said to us, "When you come to San Pat again, you shall have your cocktails, if I have to buy every rooster in San Pat County."

CHAPTER THIRTEEN

MISCELLANEOUS ADVENTURES

The Swift Murder — In the year 1874 a family by the name of Swift[88] lived near the old Refugio Mission in Refugio County. On June 8th of that year, Mr. Swift's neighbors were horrified to learn that Swift and his wife had been murdered and robbed the night before. An eyewitness who viewed the bodies and stated the facts said that outside the house were the bodies of Swift and his wife cut to pieces. It was all too revolting to describe.[89]

Swift was a sheep man who had been to St. Mary's the day before to dispose of his wool and brought back considerable money with him. It was found that the house had been ransacked and the money taken.

In a short time several posses were organized to hunt the murderers down. Some of them were trailed to Goliad County and were cornered in a building where they showed fight and killed one of the posse.[90] However, the posse eventually overpowered them and started to jail with them.

---

[88] Thad and Irene Swift. From "Refugio County History," Hobart Huson.

[89] Swift had been stabbed 18 times and his throat was cut. His wife was stabbed 24 times and her throat was cut.

[90] His name was Dan Holland.

However, they were met by another posse who took them away from their captors and made quick work of them.[91]

Among the leaders of the posse was a well-known man by the name of Henry Scott, a born leader. He had fought both Indians and Mexicans in his youth and was with his father in an Indian fight near the present town of Brownsville in which his father was killed and young Scott was captured by the Indians and taken to Mexico from whence he finally escaped back to Texas.[92]

Juan Flores, one of the instigators of the Swift murders, escaped to Mexico, where it was learned that he was boasting of the way he dealt with gringoes. Henry Scott sent a man named Bogus[93] to negotiate with Cortina, who was mayor of Matamoras, for the delivery of Flores.[94]

After the arrival of Bogus from the Rio Grande, Scott with a posse of men struck camp on the east bank of the Rio Grande. About midnight a skiff came to our side.

---

[91] A graphic account of this incident is told in "A Vaquero of the Brush Country." The men captured and slain were Antonio Moya and his father. They were not involved in the murders of Thad Swift and wife.

[92] Henry Scott, a rancher, was a neighbor of the Swift's and was also the captain of a band of "minutemen," vigilantes. This company of 36 men was known as Uncle Henry Scott's Minute Company. From "A Vaquero of the Brush Country." George Saunders: "I belonged to Uncle Henry Scott's Minute Company for two years. This company was organized at Mission Refugio in 1873 to protect the citizens of the border against Mexican bandits. When our company was called out for duty, we went at a moment's notice, regardless of what we were doing or where we were, and we rode with such vengeance that our company soon became a terror to the invading murderous Mexicans." From "Trail Drivers of Texas."

[93] Frank Boggus.

[94] Flores fled to the other side of the Rio Grande near Laredo. From "Refugio" by Hobart Huson.

When it landed two men with a prisoner between them stepped ashore. The prisoner was Juan Flores. One of the posse counted out five hundred dollars in gold. Flores was taken back to the scene of his crime and legally hung.[95]

I Am Raided — Shortly after the Swift murders the Mexicans made a raid on me, shooting at me twice through a window. I had been staying at my uncle's at night and one morning while crossing an open space on my way home I heard horses running. I looked up and saw about eight men running toward me. As I was on foot I realized that it was useless to run so I stood unwrapping my pistol, which was wrapped in my coat under my arm.

When they came nearer, I saw both Mexicans and Americans in the bunch. They were Henry Scott and posse. They asked me if I knew certain Mexicans, giving me their names, and I told them that I did and that they lived in town on "The Hill."[96]

I caught a horse and accompanied them to town and pointed out the men to them. They captured them, tied their arms and legs and took them away. I never saw them again nor tried to find them.[97] The men in the posse whose names I remember were Henry Scott, Duff Hale, and two of the

---

[95] Juan Flores was tried, convicted and sentenced to be hanged. His was the first legal hanging to take place in Refugio County. Judge W. L. Rea related that, "A large crowd turned out. I was present with the rest. Flores approached his end bravely and made a speech from the scaffold in which he admitted his guilt and admonished the spectators not to act as he did so that they would not come to the same end." From "Refugio" by Hobart Huson.

[96] An area west of the bluff in Corpus Christi which once was known as "Little Mexico" gradually became known as "The Hill."

[97] "The Texans responded to robbery and cruelty (as with the Swifts) with characteristic brutality. Unfortunately, this fell primarily upon the ethnic Mexicans of Texas." From "Lone Star" by T. R. Fehrenbach.

Castia[98] brothers. The others I have forgotten. Two of Henry Scott's daughters are still living in Corpus Christi and are well respected people.[99]

Mr. Roach Trusts the Wrong Man — A man named Roach once lived in that part of Corpus Christi that used to be called "The Hill" in the old days. It is still known by that name sometimes but then it was inhabited entirely by Mexicans.

Mr. Roach built a store there, a two-story building, and lived in the upper story. His business consisted of buying and selling produce and hides.

He had just bought some hides from a ranchero by the name of Black when some stockmen came armed with a search warrant and searched the hides. I was never able to learn what they discovered. When they went away after telling him nothing, Roach got uneasy and went to a policeman by the name of Basquez and told him about it. He told him to let him know anything he might hear and bring him a horse, promising to pay him well for his services.

As soon as it got dark, Roach went upstairs and began changing his clothes. Suddenly, his wife warned him to get out quick as a crowd of men were coming with the Mexican Basquez at their head. Roach looked through the window and saw that they were so close that he could not hope to escape by going down the stairs, so he jumped out the upper story window which was on the side opposite the intruders.

He ran west until he struck the chaparral on Nueces Bay and kept on until he came to our ranch, about four miles

---

[98] Castillo.

[99] Henry Scott died in Corpus Christi on Feb. 27, 1891 and was buried in Refugio.

from town. We were still up and had a lamp burning when he knocked on our door, saying, "Boys, please open the door, for God's sake."

Four of us stood with cocked sharpshooters while one opened the door, standing behind it. We beheld one of the wildest looking men we had ever seen. He was in his undershirt and drawers and they were torn to shreds. He was covered with blood and blood was running from his ears and nostrils. He was almost deaf as a result of running so fast through the chaparral, whose thorns had torn him pitifully. We thought he would choke before we could get any water down him, but at last he revived and told us his story.

Mr. Roach's Story — He explained that he had bought the hides from Black, knowing the latter to be a stockman, and not thinking that he had done any harm. He insisted on going out to Black's ranch that night, reasoning that since Black had gotten him into the trouble, he ought to be willing to help him out of it. We told him that it was a ten to one gamble that a posse would be waiting for him at the ranch, expecting him to take just such a course, and that the best thing he could do would be to go into the brush for four or five days, until they got tired of the hunt and gave it up. He agreed to this, after we had explained the situation to him.

Roach in Hiding — Just before daylight, we took him out into the thick chaparral and after providing for his wants, went away, and left him there. We put our spies to work to see what the other side was doing. We soon found out everything that was going on, discovering that they had men watching at the reef and at the river crossings, trying to apprehend him.

The next day we visited Roach and he wrote a letter to his wife, which was delivered to her by one of our boys. He advised her as to the disposition of his property, etc. Every day after that as long as he remained in the brush, we carried letters between him and his wife. At the end of five days, he told us he was ready to move whenever we said the word.

The Escape — We told him that we had had reports from our men and that they had stated that there had been no guards at the crossings for two days and nights. We agreed to start him out the next night, which we did.

That night we posted relays of scouts all the way to Herring's Ferry[100] on the Nueces with instructions to ride back and forth from the ferry to a certain point a few miles this side of the ferry, where I was to meet them with Roach. We were to take a roundabout way through the brush to the meeting point, where we would constantly meet some of the boys coming from the ferry in order to question them and make sure of Roach's safety.

When we arrived, we found everything clear. We woke the ferryman and when we had gotten about halfway across the river, we held the ferry up and told him that we were under the painful necessity of administering an oath. He gladly complied with our demand. Roach administered an oath to him under which he agreed never to divulge anything pertaining to the matter. If he ever broke this oath, we never heard anything about it. After we got a mile or two on the other side of the river, we bade Roach farewell and never saw him again.

---

[100] He was referring to O. H. Hearn's Ferry at Nuecestown.

A Thoughtful Woman — I shall never forget a strange thing that Roach said the night he came to our ranch. About the first words he uttered when he began to revive were, "thoughtful woman." We asked him what he meant and he said, "When I jumped out of the window, my wife said to me, 'Get to the Dunn boys as quickly as possible.' Had it not been for that, I wouldn't have known where to go."

News of Roach — About a year after Roach left, a butcher from Corpus Christi went to Germany for an operation. His name was August Ricklefsen and he was well known here. When he returned, we went to see him. For some reason, he had a peculiar grin on his face. At last I asked him what the occasion was for the mirth. He answered, "Where is Roach?" I was dumbfounded and asked him what he meant by that.

He stated that while on his way to Germany, he stopped at a German boarding house in St. Louis and that while he was sitting at the table who should come in and sit right down in front of him but Roach. Having heard of Roach's trouble, he pretended not to recognize him, but noticed that Roach kept his eye on him all the time. Ricklefsen[101] waited until Roach finished his meal and went outside and when he, Ricklefsen, had finished his own meal, a waiter stopped and asked him if he knew the man who had just gone out. He told the waiter "no" and the waiter explained that he had asked him because he had seen Roach looking at him and also saw him putting a pistol in his pocket.

Ricklefsen went outside and met Roach in the hall. Roach said to him, "How are you going to act in this matter, August?" Ricklefsen answered that since it was none of his business and since Roach had not violated any law, he

---

[101] Dunn spelled the name as "Rickelson."

intended to say nothing. He told Roach that he understood that he was simply trying to escape from a mob.

Roach invited Ricklefsen to his room, where he told him the whole story, explaining that he was living in a Western city and was doing well. He asked his guest to give the Dunn boys his undying gratitude.

A Cowardly Murder — Strange to say, the very night that we put Roach safely across the river, Black and his sons were both murdered by a Mexican. They were sitting on their porch talking when some Mexicans came up the steps and shot them as they sat in their chairs. Some claimed that it was stockmen who had the murder committed, but that is hard to say, as the stockmen have been accused of many things of which they were not guilty.

The Stabbing of Tom Gallagher — Tom Gallagher lived on the Oso Creek and owned considerable land there. The Mexicans were continually stealing wood from his land, although Gallagher had warned them not to do so. One day he discovered a Mexican on his property with his cart already loaded with wood and ready to start for town. Tom told him to wait and he would go with him.

Tom got down off his horse and tied the horse behind the cart, leaving his sharpshooter in his scabbard on the saddle. He began to climb on top of the wood with the Mexican. While Tom was climbing up, the Mexican pulled a knife out of his bosom and as Tom was about to sit down, the Mexican threw one arm over him, pushing him backwards and began stabbing him in the breast. He kept this up until he had stabbed him eleven times and threw him off the wagon and ran to Tom's horse and pulled out the sharpshooter.

He began snapping the gun at Tom's head when a number of cow-hunters happened along. The Mexican, seeing them, dropped the gun and ran into the brush. The cow-hunters took Gallagher home, where he recovered. The fact that he had on a heavy coat, making it difficult for the knife to penetrate deeply, saved his life.

We Hunt the Criminal — We heard nothing about the matter until night, but as soon as the news reached us we started out after the Mexican. We failed to find any trace of him that night, but the next day we put our spies to work in town on the Hill and located him in a Mexican's house. The next night we invaded the Hill and surrounded the house.

The house in question was a strong frame building with wooden shutters. There was a tall brush fence around it. We were so sure we were going to get our man that we had brought an extra horse and saddle for him to ride home to luncheon with us. We tied the horses to fence posts and went inside the enclosure, stationing men near the doors and windows.

Some of our men went to the front door and called the Mexican, informing him that he was under arrest. He said, "All right." We noticed the door opening slowly and in a second a hand appeared with a nickel plated pistol in it. We leaned flat against the wall. Someone shot the pistol out of his hand. The screaming of women and children and the yelling of men was something terrible.

The boys at the other windows and doors commenced firing inside. The Mexicans answered our fire, and there was so much smoke and confusion that we could see nothing. Firing also began from the other houses. We could hear the police coming, blowing their whistles, so we adjourned the meeting. When we got outside, we noticed that the horse that we had brought for our intended prisoner had broken loose and had gone, saddle and all. We went home.

The Casualties — The next morning when we got out of bed, we noticed the horse grazing in front of the house with the saddle on. Later in the day, we sent a courier to town to learn of the casualties, which were as follows: One Mexican shot through the hand, another shot through the wrist, another shot through the shoulder, two women with flesh wounds, and the house perforated with bullets. The man who had stabbed Gallagher was not touched at all, and made a clean getaway, for the time being.

The Burning of Old Man Murdoc on the Oso — Mr. Murdoc lived on the Oso about ten miles from town and nearly two miles from the Oso settlement. He lived alone in a large frame house on the Brownsville Road and sold water from a well on the road to travelers. This was his only source of income. One morning some of the people at the Oso settlement noticed a heavy smoke around his place. They paid little attention to it at first, as prairie fires were very common. A little later, looking that way after the smoke had shifted somewhat, they saw that Murdoc's house was missing.

They went to his place and found the house nothing but a heap of ashes. In searching through the ashes, they found the iron of his bedstead, a long chain, the iron teeth of a harrow with some of the teeth still in the links of the chain, and under this, they found the old man's heart which did not burn, as it was full of blood. The rest of the body, they did not find, as it had been burned to ashes.[102]

---

[102] William Murdock, an elderly man, who lived west of Corpus Christi, was killed on Aug. 19, 1872 when he was bound hand and foot, a heavy plow harrow placed on him, and his house set afire. The report

When we captured the Peñascal murderers some time afterwards they gave us the names of the members of the band that had committed this outrage and also the details of the torture of the poor old man, which were as follows:

A Gruesome Story — This band learned that Murdoc was a miser and had money hidden in the house. So they went to him and demanded it. He told them that he had but eight dollars and got it and gave it to them. They told him that he was lying and threatened to burn him if he did not produce more money. He told them that he had no more. They dragged in an old harrow and laid it on the bed, teeth up, and stretched him on top of the teeth. They fastened him with some rope and a chain.

Then began a horrible torture. First they burned the bottoms of his feet but could not get anything out of him. They set fire to the bed and went outside and fired the house in several places and left for Mexico.

There they remained a short while and then returned. As a rule such fugitives always tried to get back in time to sell their votes in the elections, knowing they would be safe as long as they stayed on the Hill. Nevertheless, the Avenging Angel often swooped down on them and spirited them away and the next election found them among the missing.

---

in the Corpus Christi newspaper said: "Murder most foul, Robbery! Arson! Prowling Mexicans, the murderers, and incendiaries. The fiends mounted and armed. Unparalleled outrages and atrocious murder within 12 miles of our city. Our blood curdles with horror and indignation as we, in duty bound, are obliged to report the facts of the most brutal outrage and atrocious murder ever committed in Western Texas. . ." From The Nueces Valley, Aug. 24, 1872.

We Observe Suspicious Actions — One day we noticed several groups of Mexicans who acted suspiciously. So that night we held our herd several miles from the road. We had with us a negro boy whom we called Black Pat.[103] The night before, he had set fire to several rats' nests, causing the rats to run out and climb bushes, where he would shoot them with an old Southern Derringer[104] he carried.

This night we told him not to set fire to the rats' nests. It was dark and we had finished our supper and were sitting around our campfire when we noticed a blaze a few hundred yards from camp. With that, we all arose and began securing our guns, when Pat came shuffling into camp laughing.

Pat Fires an Eagle's Nest — We asked him the cause of the fire and he explained that he had fired the nest of a Mexican eagle. It was a large nest made out of wood and limbs of trees and was in the top of a tall mesquite tree. The blaze lit the country for miles around. Pat's excuse was that although we had told him not to set fire to rats' nests we had said nothing about eagles' nests.

The Intruder — Our fire was in the bed of a dry creek and we were all stretched out on our blankets when we heard something coming into camp. We sat up with our hands on our sharpshooters, waiting. When the thing came into the light of the fire, we saw that it was a negro. He looked to be about six feet tall and kept coming straight towards us. I

---

[103] The practice of attaching "black" to an African-American servant's name was rather common then. Mrs. E. D. Sidbury, who was captured in the Nuecestown Raid, called her driver "Black Santos."

[104] The Southern Derringer was a small pocket pistol with the name engraved on the barrel. From the American Rifleman.

called out, "Who is that?" and the intruder sniggered and replied, "I is a man, I is." I asked, "What do you want?"

With that there was a noise just behind him that we mistook for another person, and at that moment the negro wheeled and ran, tumbling into a large chaparral bush, where the whole crowd fired at him. We were sure that we had got him, until next morning at daylight when we searched the bushes and found nothing, not even blood. But he had surely torn up the bushes in making his escape.

We Find Our Nocturnal Visitor — We now started out to see if we could locate him. About two miles further, we found a drove of sheep with a negro herding them. As soon as I spotted him, I recognized our unwelcome guest of the night before and, riding up to him, I asked him what he had wanted in our camp at night. He replied, "I wasn't in you all's camp." I told him that he was a liar and that if he told any more lies, we would swing him up. He asked us if we "wuz the gemmums camped down to the crick," and we told him we were. He said, "I seen the light of you all's fire and went down to your camp to get a piece of meat and when you all began fumblin' with them carbines I jest couldn't talk." I replied, "But you certainly did run a pretty good lick," and he said, "Oh, no suh, I just run out to that ar mott and sot down till daybreak." The mott he referred to was Mott Redondo and was about four miles from where the shooting took place.

Black Pat was very particular about fires after that. For a long time after the incident occurred he would say, if the night was very dark, "Does you all think another nigger will come into camp tonight?" Afterwards we learned that the big negro was an idiot who herded sheep for a man named Black.

143

A Peculiar Sound — One night while we were hunting the Mexican who stabbed Tom Gallagher, George Dunn and I happened to be riding in the rear of the column. We were on our way to town and on the Brownsville Road. Suddenly, George said to me, "Listen, what is that?" I stopped and listened a moment and caught the sound of a faint bell. It sounded just like the small bell used by the priests in the church service and was so different from any bell we had ever heard on the prairie that we decided to investigate.

The chaparral was so dense in the direction of the sound that we could not penetrate it on horseback, so we tied our horses and walked and crawled until we came upon a bunch of burros hobbled in the chaparral. We squatted down and rested a few moments. All at once George grabbed my arm and whispered, "look there."

We Find Smugglers — I looked in the direction he pointed and saw what looked like a fire, which seemed to be not more than 25 or 30 feet from where we were sitting. However, just before we arrived there we found this distance to be over 100 yards. When we got within twenty feet of the light, it blazed up for a moment and we could see the outlines of two men lying on separate blankets about ten feet apart. They were sound asleep. Just on one side of them was a large pile of objects that we mistook for green hides. The idea came to us at once that they had been killing cattle for their hides, which at that time was a common practice.

I whispered to George and told him to crawl to the one on the left, and to jump astraddle of him with his pistol in his hand, while I attended to the other one. When George straddled his man the latter bucked so hard that George had to clip him on the head to quieten him down. My man was better disposed and began to beg for mercy.

We asked if they had hides in the bundles and they said "yes." Thereupon we examined the bundles and found that they contained "mescal" in goat hides and crates of fine Mexican hats. Our prisoners confessed that they were smugglers and gave us all the mescal we could drink. When we started they asked us if we were not going to take anything. We told them no.

Falsely Accused — Thereupon, one of them opened a crate of hats and taking the hat off of my head put one of the fine Mexican hats on it, and thanked us for our forbearance. The next morning I happened to be in town wearing the hat when a policeman came up to me and told me that I had better get out of town. I asked him why. He told me that two Mexicans had sworn out a warrant for me and another man (meaning George), saying that we had robbed their camp and had taken a fine Mexican hat from them, and that they had my hat to prove it by.

Vindicated — I went home and got several of the boys to ride out to their camp and pretend that they were hunting two men who had stolen horses from them, describing George and me as the thieves. The Mexicans swallowed this story hook, line and sinker, and told them that the men they were hunting were in their camp the previous night and had drunk their mescal and taken a fine hat from them. The boys asked them if they would help to hang the two men if they caught them and they said that nothing would give them more pleasure.

The boys reported that the camp was empty, nothing there but their saddles, as the plunder had already been delivered. The next night, the boys took us to the camp, to be identified, but as soon as the Mexicans looked at us, they said that we had never taken a single thing and that they had to force the hat on me. However, I put a rope around the Mexican's neck and quirted[105] him until my arm ached. George and I could have reported them and would have been entitled to half the proceeds, which would have amounted to about two hundred dollars, but we would not give them away. We were sorry afterwards that we did not report them and had but little respect for smugglers thenceforward.

I Bargain for Cattle — In the years 1874 and 1875 there lived an old Mexican rancher on the Banquete Creek, 25 miles from Corpus Christi, named Nicolas Garcia. He had two sons who were regular devils. They had been implicated in the murder of several Americans and were hiding out for it.

The old man had a nice little herd of cattle which I heard he was offering at a sacrifice, as he intended leaving also. As I was in the stock business, I went one morning and talked to him about buying his stock. His brand was the shape of a gourd.

Nicolas stated that his wife had an interest in the stock and that she used the same brand, but that her earmark was different from his. I closed the trade with him and told him to be at H. L. Dreyer's stall in the City Market at 4 o'clock, as I had my money in Dreyer's safe.

I arrived at the market about ten minutes to 4 and Garcia arrived a few minutes later. We sat down on one of the benches in the stall and were talking about the stock. I had forgotten the difference in the earmarks, so I got off the

---

[105] Lashed with a quirt, a short leather whip made with a stock filled with lead.

bench and squatted down on the floor to draw a diagram of the marks and told him to show me the difference.

He slid off the bench and snapped a pistol at my breast, saying, "Here it is."

The pistol failed to fire, as it had doubtless been loaded a long time and had gotten damp. I grabbed him by the collar and stuck my pistol to his breast and let it go.

Exciting Moments — It was like holding a cat by the tail. He would jump between my legs and up into the air like a trained rooster. I had fired three shots at him and the thought struck me that I would soon be covered with blood if I did not get rid of him. So I flung him away from me and started to go out through the front of the market.

I had gotten about halfway when someone grabbed me by the collar and I felt something cold at the back of my neck. When I turned around, I was surprised to find old Nicolas still frolicking with me. I grabbed the pistol and jerked it out of his hand and discovered why he had not been killed by my first shot. The pistol was in his bosom and I had struck it and torn it up pretty badly. The mainspring was shot from under the hammer, the wooden handle was entirely off and part of the hammer was gone. I also discovered that this was a different pistol from the first one he had snapped at me.

I threw the pistol over a stall and turned to walk out after again throwing Garcia away from me, but I opened fire on him again, as he ran through the market. When he got outside, he ran down the sidewalk to where the State National Bank is now. Kneeling on the sidewalk, I took deliberate aim at him, trying to plug him between the shoulders, but he seemed to bear a charmed life.

Just as he got under the porch of the building on the corner, the police grabbed him and took him to jail. I was indicted for the matter, however, and Garcia was not indicted at all. But the jury acquitted me without leaving the box. Old man Garcia left here and went to Falfurrias, where he died a few years ago.

Miguel Carries a Gun for Me — In the old days it was customary when we went on a cow-hunt for each one to chip in and pay for his share of the provisions. Each one also helped to pay the cook as well as to pay an extra share for each hand he brought along.

On the particular occasion I am going to describe, one of the boys had a Mexican named Miguel working for him. Miguel brought with him a musket which he carried in front of him on the saddle every day. We could not understand why he did this so I sent a negro boy to question him and find out what I could. He told the negro that he had heard that I was a bad man and that he was watching me.

We had rounded up some wild cattle that day and among them were some fighting bulls. I had shot every cartridge that I had at them and so had most of the boys. However, one of us had an old Southern Derringer, which shot a cartridge about half the length of my own pistol. I borrowed three cartridges from the owner of the derringer. I was not sure whether they would shoot or not but I made up my mind that Miguel would be minus a musket in the morning.

I observed that at night he always laid the musket lengthwise on the bed where he slept. This night it was pretty cool, so he spread his blanket near the wagon tongue and went to sleep.

After making sure that he was asleep, myself and a fellow named Jerry spread our blankets on the other side of the tongue from him. We took a long branding hook and hooked it into the guard of the musket, pulling it slowly into the fire, at the same time moving the barrel so that it would not strike any one when it went off. We moved the butt of the musket in first, up to where the barrel was fastened to the stock. We moved our blankets to another place and waited for the fireworks.

A Miniature Earthquake — We did not have long to wait for the noise the gun made when it exploded sounded as if it were loaded with TNT. It blew the fire in all directions and went straight up in the air where the barrel parted company with the stock and, whirling over and over several times, stuck straight up in the ground.

In a few seconds everyone was out of bed with their guns cocked, asking what had happened. If Miguel suspected anything, he said nothing.

A "Bad Nigger Killer" from Austin — The next morning we took our cattle to town and disposed of them, after which Pat Dunn and I started for our ranches four miles from town. Just about two hundred yards from where the road to Laredo branches off, a young man overtook us. He introduced himself as a "bad nigger killer from Austin," stating that he had made a specialty of shooting negroes on foot logs on the Colorado River for the past five years.

Trouble with the Negro Leonard — While we were talking, some wagons loaded with wood came driving by. Someone on them said something to Pat, which I did not hear. Pat, however, turned on the Mexican driver and gave him a beating with his quirt. Pat rode on ahead of me and the bad man. Just as we got to the top of what is called Tom Whalen's Hill, the man said, "Look, that nigger is going to kill that boy."

I saw three wagons loaded with lumber and goods and driven by negroes. Pat was riding alongside one of the wagons, whipping a negro who was pulling at a musket that was fastened under some quilts and plunder. When I came up I said, "Here, don't shoot that boy!" He replied, "I will shoot you, you" — (calling me a foul name). I said, "Don't try to joke with me," and shot my pistol in his face but somehow missed him. By that time he had given the musket a hard jerk and got it loose.

My horse, being very spirited, was cutting up so that it was impossible to take aim. When the negro got the gun loose, he jumped off the wagon inside a pasture and raised the gun to shoot me. The wagon wheel struck my horse and made it rear straight up. This gave me a chance to draw a good bead on the negro and hit him over the left eye. I saw the ball kick up dirt on the other side of him. When the battle was over, I saw that I was alone. The bad man from Austin had dissolved into space and I never saw him again.

Acquitted — The cartridge that struck the negro was a small Colt Derringer cartridge. One would think to look at it that it would hardly go through a shingle.

When the performance was over, I told the negro drivers to move on, as I wanted the body to lie in the same position that it fell in, until the inquest was over. I started on my way.

I happened to look back and saw that all the drivers were stopped around the dead negro. When they saw me, they broke for the brush, but I rounded them up again and made them mount their wagons and move on.

The coroner's jury brought in a verdict of justifiable homicide. A year later another jury brought in a verdict of murder in the first degree, but it amounted to nothing, for the final jury acquitted me without leaving the box.

The Murder of Tom Shaw — Tom Shaw was a Corpus boy who was raised in the city. One day[106] the sheriff here received a message from the sheriff of Live Oak County that he had arrested a Mexican called Martine[107] who was wanted in Corpus, and that he would hold him at Los Olmos Ranch until a deputy arrived.

The sheriff appointed Tom Shaw a deputy and sent him after Martine. When he arrived there, Martine proposed that they all go to Corpus in his ambulance as he wanted to bring his wife and family with him.

The sheriff of Live Oak County tried to persuade Shaw not to go in the ambulance, but Shaw stated that he would be in no danger as he was well acquainted with Martine. So Shaw tied his horse behind the ambulance and sat on the front seat with Martine, the family sitting on the rear seat.

Within a few miles from Los Olmos, Martine asked Shaw to drive the ambulance while he rolled a cigarette. Pretending to be reaching for his tobacco pouch, he pulled out a large double edged dirk and drove it through Shaw's back and out through his breast. He stabbed him in a dozen places and threw him out of the ambulance. The murderer changed his route for Mexico and was missed ever afterwards at the polls.

Murder of Lee Rabb — The Rabb ranch was situated on Banquete Creek and was owned by Mrs. Rabb and her three sons, Dock, Frank, and Lee. Their cattle and horses were branded with the famous bow and arrow brand.

One night there was a Mexican dance at Petronila and Lee Rabb had taken a Mexican girl to the entertainment. After dancing awhile the couple ordered a cup of coffee

---

[106] Sept. 12, 1877. From the Corpus Christi Weekly Gazette.
[107] His name was Martin Rodriguez.

and while they were drinking it, someone slipped up to an open window behind Lee and shot him in the back, killing him instantly. He stole one of Lee's horses and left. Some say that he was caught and killed on the banks of the Rio Grande and dumped into the river, but the know-it-alls say that he was never caught. However, he was missing at all the elections since. [108] [109]

Death of Jim Walker — Another officer that we lost while in the performance of his duty was Jim Walker. He arrested a Mexican by the name of Juan Palmoa at a ranch west of Corpus Christi and started to jail with him. The Mexican watched his chance and, catching Walker off his guard, snatched his pistol out of the scabbard and, shooting Walker to death, escaped.

---

[108] Dunn doesn't say so, but he may have been a member of the posse that trailed the suspect to the Rio Grande.

[109] The Lee Rabb affair was brought up in testimony before the House Committee on Military Affairs in 1878. The testimony was made by a Brownsville banker and contractor about conditions in South Texas: "This man (Lee) Rabb was a desperado and a murderer and was the terror of his neighbors, often of his friends. He became involved in a difficulty with some men said to be Mexicans and he was killed." Q. "What took place after that?" A. "His so-called friends, men living in that country, banded together and killed quite a number of innocent Mexicans." Q. "How many?" A. "I should say not less than forty." . . . Q. "Were they killed indiscriminately, just as the bands came upon them, or were they men who were selected to be killed?" A. "It is reported that the bands killed them just as they came across them." From "An American-Mexican Frontier: Nueces County Texas" by Paul Shuster Taylor.

CHAPTER FOURTEEN

MY LATER LIFE

Refugees in Texas — On the 19th of June 1867, the Emperor Maximilian of Mexico was executed. His army was composed of Belgians, Austrians and French. Most of his garrisons on the border towns crossed the Rio Grande into the United States. Quite a number came to Corpus Christi.

After their arrival here, the various nationalities paired off themselves. The Belgians located on the lot where the parsonage of the Methodist Church now stands. At that time, there were three or four concrete houses on the place which belonged to an old lady named McComb. The Belgians opened an oyster saloon and a restaurant in one of the houses, and in the other they made and sold a kind of home brew that they had learned to make in Belgium.

At that time I was working with my uncle five miles from town. One of the Belgians came there and was employed by my uncle. His name was August Vandavell. We became great friends. We used to go to town on Sundays and eat dinner with his countrymen.

A Tale of Waterloo — Among them was a man who had been badly wounded in the shoulder while in Mexico. He was unable to work and on Sundays everyone would chip in and make up a purse to keep him during the week. Being a guest, I was more than glad to contribute my part also.

The wounded man's name was Louis Capella and he had held some office in Maximilian's army, the rank of which I have forgotten. He seemed to appreciate what I had done for him and afterwards proved that he did by more than repaying my small favors.

One Sunday, we were looking over some magazines and at one in particular that had a cut of the battlefield of Waterloo. The wounded man seemed to be very excited about the picture and as the crowd gathered around the table, he pointed out the different localities on the field. After the excitement had died down, I asked him if he had ever seen the battlefield, and he stated that he had played on it as a boy. It seemed that a relative of his owned the small farm there when the battle was fought and after it was over and the farmers returned to their homes, most of them took their drays and loaded them up with plunder from the field. This they stowed in their homes and cellars and afterwards sold to tourists for a good price.

He said that the next year after the battle, his relative bought all the relics he could from the other farmers and opened a museum in Antwerp. He said to me, "If I ever get home, I'll send you a souvenir of the battle."

Capella Keeps His Promise — In the meantime, the yellow fever scourge swept over the city and a great many of the Belgians died. Among them was August Vandavella who was working at my uncle's ranch. As I had not afterwards seen any of the others, I supposed that they had all died with the yellow fever.

Nearly two years afterward a large schooner from New York came to the wharf here and the ship's carpenter came ashore hunting me. He was a Dane by the name of Poulsin.

When I heard that he was looking for me, I went aboard and found him. He told me that a friend of his in Antwerp had sent me a present by him.

He opened a chest and brought out a piece of exploded bombshell as large as my hand. There was a letter with it, but it was written in Belgian and I was unable to read it. On leaving the vessel, I almost threw the present into the bay as I did not know its value and thought a joke had been played on me.

The Origin of My Museum — I looked up a Belgian who was a bookkeeper for a local firm and asked him to translate the letter into English for me. It read as follows:

"This is part of a bombshell fired by Napoleon's artillery at Waterloo, June 18th, 1815. The bomb struck the Château Hougoumont which was occupied by the British troops. There it exploded. Presented by Louis Capella, a native of Belgium, and a member of Maximilian's army in Mexico in 1867." About two years after he sent me the shell, he sent me a sword from Waterloo that had been used by one of Blucher's dragoons in the battle, and after that he sent me a couple of pistols.[110]

These generous gifts awakened my interest in the collection of war relics and I began collecting souvenirs from all the different wars and have been engaged in doing so ever since. In addition to war relics I have a great deal of native stuff from the Philippines, Borneo, Admiralty Isles and various other places. I also have a nice collection of Indian relics to which I have been adding all the time and

---

[110] Felix von Blucher, a Corpus Christi pioneer and early Nueces County surveyor, was a grandnephew of the Prussian general at Waterloo, Gehard Lebrecht von Blucher. From "Maria von Blucher's Corpus Christi" edited by Bruce S. Cheeseman.

have souvenirs from forty-eight different battles and sectors in France and Belgium.

My Marriage and Family — In the year 1878, I was married to Mrs. Lelia Nias of Springfield, Mo., after which I engaged in the farming and dairy business. After a few years, I opened the Crescent Hotel in Corpus Christi but after a year I gave up that business and returned to the farm on the same tract of land that Col. H. L. Kinney had presented to my father. In 1880, our son John, now deceased, was born, and in 1894 our daughter Maude.

John had two children, Earl and John Marvin. Both boys have served a term in the United States Navy, previous to which they served in the National Guard. Both boys are now married and are living in Corpus Christi. My daughter, Maude, after teaching for three years in the high schools of Texas, held various positions of responsibility in the business world. She has had a university education and founded and conducted the Academy of Commerce and Languages in Mexico, chartered by Governor Treviño of Coahuila. She has now married and has entered the literary profession, where she has gained considerable recognition, her poetry having appeared in numerous poetry journals throughout the United States, and in various anthologies, and her fiction having been published in several national magazines. She is the vice-president of the International Scientific Association.

I have now retired from business, having reached the age of eighty years, but am still interested in the collection of historical relics for my museum on the Shell Road, a museum which contains perhaps the largest private collection of its kind in the United States.[111]

---

[111] See Appendix Four.

Captain Richard King — Captain King of Santa Gertrudis Ranch was one of the wealthiest men in this section. His herds grazed on thousands of acres of free domain. He and his partner Captain Kenedy owned and operated one or more steamboats on the Rio Grande. Captain King always stood for progress and his presence in this section was a public boon.

In those days herds were driven overland to Kansas to market and King and Kenedy were perhaps the largest shippers in the state. During the war the enemy made a special raid from Brazos Santiago to his ranch home to capture him. The captain was absent at the time but in the early morning, the prowlers saw a servant on the gallery and without a word of warning shot the man to death, thus showing their fear of the one they sought.[112]

Captain King's life reads like a romance and if told to the letter, it would not be credited.

Once when the captain was in Corpus he hired a newly landed German to drive his carriage. When they left the city they drove to Petronila Creek and stopped for lunch, on the near side of the stream. After an hour's rest they started out again, and as they breasted the opposite bank, shots were fired from ambush, the German driver being instantly killed.[113]

With that the horses broke and ran but fortunately kept the road to the ranch. Four Mexicans rode out of the bushes and gave a wild chase, taking care, however, to keep out of the range of the captain's Winchester. When they neared

---

[112] The man killed was a house servant, Francisco Alvarado, who ran out and yelled, "Don't fire on this house. There is family here." He was shot dead on the front porch. From "The King Ranch" by Tom Lea.

[113] His name was Franz Specht; he was was a traveler who asked for a ride to Brownsville. The driver of King's carriage was George Evans. From "The King Ranch" by Tom Lea.

the ranch, the Mexicans wheeled and went just as fast in the other direction. This was only one of Captain King's hairbreadth escapes.[114]

We Revisit Old Scenes and are Pleasantly Entertained — In the year 1930 myself and my brother Matt, while riding across the country, came in sight of the King Ranch. It was the first time I had seen it since 1875.

It seemed to me as if the old ranch was beckoning to us to come on and I suggested to Matt that we go there. When we arrived at the ranch, we learned from a conversation with some of the employees that Mr. Kleberg was confined to his bed and had been for some time. The man asked us if we would like to go in and see him and we said yes, if it would not cause any inconvenience.

He asked us to wait a moment and very soon a young lady, a daughter of Mr. and Mrs. Kleberg, came downstairs and introduced herself to us saying that her father would be very pleased to see us. She escorted us upstairs to her father and mother and it was more like meeting relatives than friends. We talked over the old times when the captain was alive in the those troublesome days and perilous times of the 1870s.

---

[114] The details of the attack on King's carriage on July 30, 1872, on San Fernando Creek, are included in the Robb Commission report. The U.S. Commissioners investigated violent and lawless conditions in South Texas. King was on his way to testify before the commission in Brownsville when the attack was made. From the Report of the United States Commissioners to Texas, Dec. 10, 1872.

APPENDICES

MISCELLANEOUS RECOLLECTIONS OF JOHN B. DUNN

My father came to Corpus Christi with the Army of Occupation, with Zachary Taylor. He was sutler for the troops, and went on from here to Brownsville with Taylor. After the battles of Resaca de la Palma, Buena Vista, and Palo Alto, he enlisted as a teamster so as to get across the river, as no civilians were allowed to cross. In the hills around Monterrey he was attacked by lancers, but beat his way back into camp. Taylor appointed him a courier and dispatch bearer for the army. He served several years in Mexico.

Colonel Kinney told my father he would give him one hundred acres of land if he would built out on this road (Shell Road). He did, engaging in farming and raising stock. One day he became overheated in the field and was ill. He was sent to New Orleans for treatment, and later was taken to Baton Rouge. My mother was very poor and very much broken up over this trouble. She struggled to pay all she could for his care. After father was sent to Baton Rouge, all trace of him was lost; hunting of records showed nothing; we were never able to trace him.

My mother was Sarah Pritchett, who was related to the Mussetts.

There were a great many Dunns in and around Corpus Christi. There were two Lawrence Dunns. One was a brother of Pat Dunn; he was so tall he couldn't ride an ordinary horse but had to have an extra large one. I guess he was the tallest man in Texas, as he was over seven feet. The other Larry Dunn was a brother of cousin John; he lived on Padre Island. He was killed by Mexicans at Petronila under a flag of truce, but he didn't leave a wife and children, as stated by one writer, for he never even had a family. This writer doesn't even tell exactly how he was killed.

Colonel Kinney was still living when I was a small child, but I don't remember a great deal about him. I do remember the Sunday afternoon cockfights that took place at my father's place out in the country. My father took care of Kinney's fighting cocks. On Sunday afternoon Kinney would ride out there with a lot of Mexicans; he carried his little daughter on his horse in front of him.

There was one time in the early fifties that Kinney was penning a lot of mustangs up there on the Rincon. Right outside the bayou there was a mustang pen made of big tall fences. Kinney would kill the mustangs for their hides. He would go out and rodeo them, and run them into the Rincon, and then put them in the pens. One day the men heard a noise up near the river, and found out it was a bunch of Indians coming. The men fell back into some mesquites that were up there where Taylor's breastworks were. The Indians came by on a run and probably didn't see them. The Indians went on and when they came to the bayou they threw their buffalo robes in, so the horses wouldn't sink in the mud. They were Comanches, about eight or ten in the bunch. Kinney and his men fired on them from the mesquites, but missed them. There was a big chase that led out west of town a few miles to a mott of live oak trees. Here an old man killed one of the Indians. This place ought to have a marker.

Another place that ought to have a historical marker is Grulla Motts, on the Oso. Matt Dunn said the ranch originally belonged to Mustang Gray, who sold it to Sam Glen, who was a caporal for Rabb's Ranch. I think he sold it to George Pettigrew. It should have markers on it because Mustang Gray was so famous as a ranger.

Colonel Kinney was in Matamoros when he was killed. Julius Henry told me he lifted Kinney up after he was shot, assisted by Martin Hinojosa, and removed his pistol. I have this pistol in my museum.

A long time ago my mother told me that the way Corpus Christi got its name was that Aubrey and Kinney were arguing one day, saying it was time get a post office here, and that someone said, "What will we name it?" Kinney said, "Why, since the bay is named Corpus Christi, we could call it Corpus Christi."

Another thing that I have been told was about the bombardment of this town during the Civil War. We were living at Gonzales then, but this story was told me by Julius Henry and Chris Yung. The first or the second shell that came into Corpus Christi struck Mr. Shaw's saloon. It tore into the gable of the building and went through the counter, tearing bottles off the shelves and killing a Newfoundland dog. Then it bounced across the street and rolled up to Mrs. Allen's house (she was the mother of Mary Allen), and stopped against a fence. I call that the Carrie Nation shell because it liberated some liquor. You know, some of those shells had whiskey in them.

In later years, Mrs. Allen sent me word to come get that shell, and get it quick. I asked her what was the matter with it, and she said she had just read in a San Antonio paper that a shell which had been lying around since the Civil

War and used to support a wash kettle, had exploded and killed a woman and two children. I have that shell of Mrs. Allen's in my museum.

These breastworks up on the north beach were made by Zachary Taylor's men. They thought maybe the Mexicans would attack them here, and they wanted to be prepared.

You ask what a roly barrel was? It was a round barrel hauled along by means of a rope, rolling as it went. People would fill these roly barrels with water from one of the full cisterns, during time of a drought, and sell the water. John Woessner got his start with a roly barrel.

Yes, I recall a Mr. Dougherty of Brownsville. He was a prominent member of the Red Men, and I used to meet him at the Great Councils.

Gussettville was opposite Fort Merrill on the Nueces River. I camped there many and many a time, but I can't recollect just where it was, now. The changing of the names of these old places puts a person at sea.

John Dunn was interviewed for his recollections by Marie Blucher. Dates of interviews: May 11 and May 29, 1939, and June 21, 1940. Mr. Dunn died Nov. 3, 1940 at the age of 89 years.

APPENDIX TWO

For a comprehensive sketch of my museum I quote verbatim an article recently published in a local Corpus Christi paper, *The South Texas News:*

Dunn's Museum Recreates the Days When Men Lived in Danger in the Corpus Christi Region — Wouldn't it be wonderful if we moderns could travel back in time on some carpet of Baghdad to those thrilling days when the "vaqueros" roamed through the chaparral and the romantic rangers battled to hold our Southern boundary against the periodic depredations of the Mexican raiders?

Very few people of South Texas realize that such a magic carpet is actually available to them. It is only necessary to step into Dunn's historical museum on the Shell Road two miles west of Corpus Christi to find oneself instantly back in the past surrounded by the martial paraphernalia of the times when men followed Nietzche's advice[115] and "lived dangerously," J. B. Dunn is one of the oldest living pioneers of the Corpus Christi section. He has worked for over fifty years collecting relics and souvenirs of our historic past and preserving them for future generations. He has the largest private collection of this kind in Texas, perhaps in the United States.

He specializes in the collection of firearms of all ages of the world and has souvenirs of all wars and all important battlefields from the days of Napoleon down to and including the World War. His Indian collection is particularly interesting and he has even reached over into ancient Egypt and the Orient and into all the strange dark corners of the earth and brought back treasures impregnated with the fragrance of mysterious lands and races little known.

---

[115] "The secret of the greatest fruitfulness and the greatest enjoyment of existence is to live dangerously." Friedrich Nietzche, "The Joyful Wisdom."

He has received numerous substantial offers to travel with his museum or to locate in more populous sections. These offers he has steadfastly refused for he is of that stoic type to whom the glitter of gold is less brilliant than the lure of the home land.

He himself was an actual participant in the thrilling battles of the early days. Some of the fire arms in his museum were captured with his own hands from noted bandits and murderers who once spread terror through the homes, of peaceful rangers. Among these weapons might be mentioned the ornate pistol of Hypolita Tapia, Mexican bandit, who with his gang robbed the store at Peñascal and committed four murders back in 1874.

He also cherishes the Winchester that he carried while a member of Chamberlain's company of rangers in 1870 and a Sharp's carbine that he used in Wallace's company in 1874.

Among other relics of particular interest to the people of Corpus Christi section, one might mention: A pistol found in the pocket of Col. Kinney when he was killed in a Mexican revolution where he had taken sides. This pistol was presented to Mr. Dunn by a brother-in-law of the Colonel. Kinney will be remembered as the founder of Corpus Christi and was a personal friend and associate of Mr. Dunn's father to whom he presented one hundred acres of land west of Corpus Christi. Part of this land still constitutes Mr. Dunn's homestead and is known as Kinney Park in honor of Corpus Christi's adventurous founder.

An iron chain with which Mr. Murdoc of the Oso community was tied before being robbed and burned to death by Mexican bandits about the year 1873.

An elaborate pistol belonging to Cortina, famous border bandit who afterwards became a general in the Mexican army and mayor of Matamoras.

A Russian samovar washed off a ship on Padre Island. This huge brass vessel carries inscriptions and regal coats of arms showing that it has taken premiums in practically every capital in Europe.

An ancient flint-lock belonging to Conrad Meuly, pioneer of Corpus Christi.

A naval sword belonging to an officer in the company of the Federal Commander, Captain Kittredge, surrendered when the latter was captured by Confederate troops at Flour Bluff.

Numerous bomb-shells fired into Corpus Christi by the Federal troops during the two bombardments of the city in 1862.

An ancient crane on which pioneers of this section used to hang their kettles.

Hundreds of Indian arrowheads and several flint axes found in Nueces County.

A musket and some cannon balls picked up on the site of General Taylor's breastworks located near the present causeway.

Among the hundreds of foreign relics which adorn the museum might be enumerated:

An Oriental blunderbuss over two hundred years old, engraved with verses from the Koran.

Part of an exploded shell from the battlefield of Waterloo, presented to Mr. Dunn by an officer in Maximilian's army, whose parents lived on that historic spot. It might be interesting to note that this relic was the first souvenir in the collection and was the origin of Mr. Dunn's interest in the acquisition of historical relics.

Chinese matchlock, dated 1620.

Chinese headman's knife used in the Boxer Uprising.

A coin of Caesar's time.

The hand of an Egyptian mummy.

Besides being a mere collector, Mr. Dunn, despite his eighty years, is tireless in the field of archeological excavation on the sites of the historical landmarks of Corpus Christi, and vicinity. Only recently his efforts were rewarded when he unearthed the skeleton of an Indian girl on which he found a magnificent necklace and a bracelet both of pearl shells. This skeleton was discovered, along with many others, on the site of what must have been an ancient burial ground, at the mouth of what is called the "blind Oso," a branch of the Oso creek.

A few years ago, while excavating on the site of an Indian battleground at the mouth of the Oso, Mr. Dunn dug up a silver-handled sword engraved with curious symbols. Numerous archeologists have disputed about the possible history of this weapon, as the symbols cannot be definitely associated with those of any known period. This sword with its delicate traceries constitutes one of the most unusual "finds" in the entire collection.

Free to the Public — The museum is open to the public freely at all times and undoubtedly offers a fertile field ,of research for those who would become more intimately acquainted with the colorful history of our great Southwest.

Mr. Dunn's name has been frequently mentioned in historical literature and books pertaining to the history of his times. A recent biography appearing in "The New Encyclopedia of Texas," has this to say of his father and himself, "Had it not been for such men and their sons, the southern boundary of the United States would be much nearer the latitude of 36 than 39."

— Published in *The South Texas News.*

Our Trip to Monterrey — In November 1929, my brother Matt and I took a trip to Monterrey, Mexico. I felt that I would be able to secure numerous war relics as Monterrey has been a regular incubator for revolutions in which all kinds of war munitions were used.

While there, we called on the American consul, Mr. Fitzsimmons, and he kindly furnished a guide to pilot us to all the places in the city, where we would be most likely to find any antiques, but it was like hunting a needle in a haystack. At one place which we visited, the proprietor said that he had but one rare relic for whose genuineness he could vouch. He then unlocked a drawer and taking it out began to give me the history of it. It was a late model Smith and Wesson six-shot pistol. The man stated that it was the identical pistol that Cortez carried when he invaded Mexico and the same one with which he wounded Montezuma in a poker game in the city of Mexico. He offered it to me for the low price of $6.50, but I declined purchasing until I had more thoroughly familiarized myself with the history of Mexico.

Matt Takes His Annual Bath — Our first trouble occurred when we visited the noted Topo Chico Springs. Nothing would do Matt but he must take a bath in them. I tried to reason with him but he would not listen to me. I told him that it was likely to cause complications between the two governments as the soil that was on his body was Texas soil and that one bloody war had been fought already and it would be a pity to bring on more strife when he could just as easily take a bath in Texas and leave her soil at home, but he had his own way.

I Make an Offer for the Baptismal Fount — The next false move was made by me. While in the Bishop's Palace, which General Taylor stormed and took, the caretaker, while showing us around, came to a large Baptismal Fount hewn out of a solid rock. When he came within a few feet of it, he halted, removed his hat, and crossed himself a dozen times. He told us that over two thousand Aztecs had been baptized in this fount. When he had finished his sermon, I asked him if he would take fifty cents for it.

He shook like he had the palsy and began swallowing and twitching as though he was going to have a fit. I told Matt that we had better move on, which we did.

We Hear a Bugle Call — Just as we boarded a streetcar, we heard a bugle sound and we were sure that it was a call to arms to apprehend us. However, when we got back to the Continental Hotel we found ourselves perfectly safe and outside of the fear that someone might try to collect the $500 reward offered for Lieutenant Ferguson and myself after our long past trouble with the theatrical man at Lagarto, we passed the time serenely enough. We found the Mexican people very polite and courteous on all occasions and although the city was wide open, with saloons on every block, we never, during the four days that we were there, saw a single drunk man. We may be superior to the Mexicans in some things, but in others they are superior to us.

APPENDIX FOUR

J. B. "Red" Dunn

The following pages are a reproduction of an brochure used by Dunn to promote his museum on Shell Road. Many of the photogaphs were provided by the Corpus Christi Museum of Science & History from the "Doc" Frederick McGregor collection. The John B. "Red" Dunn weapons collection is housed in the Museum.

DUNN'S MUSEUM

CENTENNIAL DISPLAY, 1936

Corpus Christi, Texas

MAKERS OF TEXAS

These are the makers of Texas
Bred where her battles were won,
Men who were bronzed by the desert,
Men who were kissed by the sun:

Men with the sea in their voices,
Prophets who forged through the night
Building in life—barren spaces,
Mansions of beauty and light.

Blazing the trails that we follow,
Down where the bluebonnets nod;
These are the makers of Texas,
Men who were chosen by God.

Lilith Lorraine

DUNN'S MUSEUM

Dunn's Museum, two miles from the city of Corpus Christi, on the Shell Road, is said to be the largest privately owned historical collection in the United States. Mr. Dunn himself, an ex-ranger who served with Wallace's and Chamberlain's Companies, is the oldest native-born pioneer of Corpus Christi, his father, Matthew Dunn, having come here with Taylor's army.

Mr. Dunn, who has worked for over fifty years in the collection of his specimens, specializes in fire arms of all ages and has souvenirs of all the important battlefields from the days of Napoleon down to and including the World War. His Indian collection is particularly extensive and has reached over to Egypt and the Orient, and into all the strange dark corners and brought back tresures impregnated with the fragrance of mysterious lands and races little known.

He himself was an actual participant in the thrilling battles of the early days, including the famous Mexican raid on Corpus Christi in 1875. Some of the firearms in his collection were captured with his own hands from noted bandits and murderers who spread terror throuh the homes of the settlers. He has loaned to the Ex-Rangers Exhibit at the Dallas Centennial the Winchester which he carried while a member of Chamberlain's Company, and a Sharp's Carbine that he used in Wallace's Company in 1874.

His memoirs, PERILOUS TRAILS OF TEXAS, written after he had passed the age of 80, related the principal events of pioneer days in which he was an actual participant.

174

BOMB AND HELMET DISPLAY

Photo number one, taken in front of Dunn's Museum shows "Red" John Dunn, the owner, with a few of the Bombs, helmets and machine guns in his huge collection. Among the helmets are two from Prussia, one from the Province of Wurtenberg, one belonging to the British Lancers, a U. S. helmet used before the Civil War, another used by the French in the Franco-Prussian War, one belonging to the Japanese, and a Mexican soldier's cap taken from Villa's troops in his raid on Juarez.

A notable machine gun is a Hotchkiss, manufactured in Detroit for the French government. This gun was once the property of the ill-fated Captain Walter Wanderwell, who was murdered aboard his yacht, Carmine, at Long Beach, California. After taking it around the world in 1920, he sold it to a dealer in San Antonio, from whom Mr. Dunn purchased it.

In the picture is also shown a Colt machine gun used by the U. S. Marines in the battle of the Marne, a German airplane gun, (Maxim) captured in 1918 by American troops, and a Vicker's airplane gun, also used in the World War.

Some of the bombs shown have a special relation to Corpus Christi, as several were fired into the harbor here by Federal troops during the Civil War. There is also an airplane bomb from Wheeler Field, the naval base at Honolulu, and a cannon shell from the U. S. S. Mine Layer, Ludlow. The tall shell with projectile came from a German submarine captured by a U. S. vessel in the World War.

All the relics shown here and thousands of other curios with historical associations will be on exhibition at Dunn's Museum near the Fred Robert's Hospital, in Corpus Christi, during the Texas Centennial celebration. Several other interesting exhibits have been loaned to the Ranger's Exhibit at Dallas and to the University of Texas.

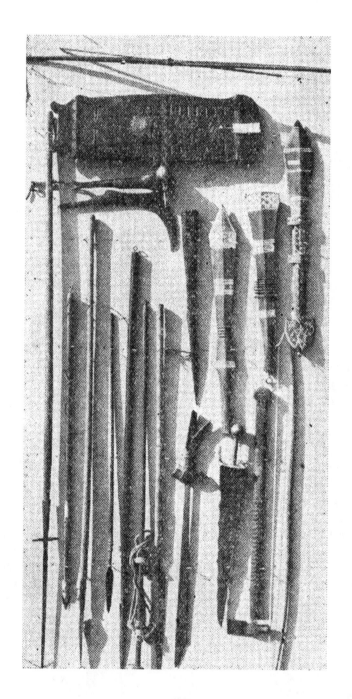

PIKE AND SPEAR DISPLAY

Photo number two is a representative display of a few of the spears, pikes, and other weapons on exhibition at Dunn's Museum on the Shell Road. Reminiscent of the War between the States is a Confederate pike made in the State of Georgia and bringing memories of nearer home is a Mexican War lance found at old San Patricio where Urrea's Lancers formed part of the garrison once stationed there.

Among the spears is one from the Malay Peninsula, a throwing spear from the Philipines, while from the far Arctic comes one used for spearing wall uses.

Keeping company with ferocious looking war clubs from the Hawaiian Islands is a barbarically ornamented shield from Borneo with its companion knife and bolo and the curious Australian boomerang.

All these relics of savagery and industry, ancient and modern, and many thousands more may be seen at Dunn's Museum.

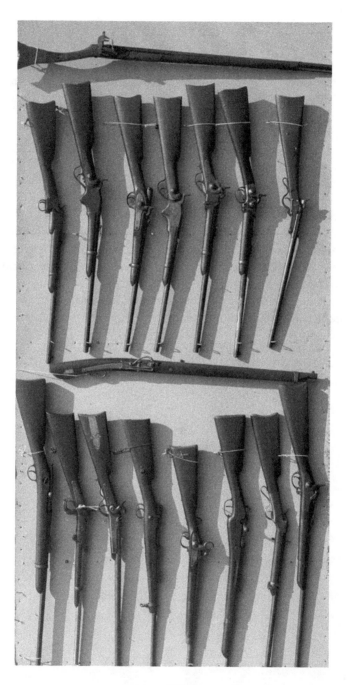

GUN DISPLAY

Photo number three shows a few of the hundreds of guns at Dunn's Museum. Of special interest to Corpus Christi and vicinity is a gun belonging to Conrad Meuly, a native of Switzerland and a pioneer of Nueces Co. Mr. Meuly was a member of the Snively Expedition which after its capture and release by Captain Philip St. George Cooke of the U. S. Dragoons, was given 10 guns to protect themselves from Indians. With his gun which was returned to him at that time, Mr. Meuly later killed two Indians in Nueces County, one at Chocolate Motts and another at the Battle of San Jacinto Ranch in which later battle Col. Kinney, founder of Corpus Christi, participated. Mr. Dunn also has a citizen rifle used by Richard Gallagher, pioneer of the Oso settlement, and another of Pat Larkin, pioneer of Corpus Christi.

Among the Civil War guns is a Sharp's Carbine from John Brown's Raid, a Tower musket used in the last battle of the Civil War fought on the old Palo Alto battleground, a Kentucky carbine used by Morgan's Raiders, a Conference Musket made in Richmond, Va., and a Maynard globe-sighted rifle used by sharpshooters. There are also Remington, Hotchkiss Burnside, Smight, Peabody and Gallagher carbines, all relics of the War Between the States.

As a reminder of Texas' struggle for independence is a citizen's rifle used in the battle of San Jacinto and a Robbins and Lawerence musket from the Mexican War. Two rifles saw service in the Spanish American war, one a Mauser and the other a Krag-Jorgensen.

In a miscellaneous display one finds a Mauser carbine used in Villa's Raid on Columbus, New Mexico, a Spencer Carbine used by Indians in the Custer Massacre, and later surrendered by them after their defeat, a musket from the Seminole War in Florida, and a buffalo gun belonging to the small band of buffalo hunters who defeated the Comanche Indians in the battle of Adobe Walls in Texas.

Among the many foreign guns might be mentioned an Austrian Army rifle, a French La Belle rifle from the Franco-Prussian War, and an Arabian Horseman's Musket.

One of the most curious of the guns is a Chinese Matchlock, dated 1816. In comparing this gun with those used in modern warfare, Mr. Dunn states that nowadays a soldier could be killed, prepared for burial and given a first class military funeral before such a gun could be brought into action.

POWDERHORN AND BLUNDERBUSS DISPLAY

Photo number four shows the powderhorn collection from the museum, which has as its principal exhibit a beautiful horn containing the words "Republic of Texas" and ornamented with the Lone Star. There is another powderhorn which was taken from an Indian killed in Montague County on Red River in a fight between Texas Rangers and Indians. The above powderhorn and several others have been loaned to the University of Texas for its Centennial Exhibit.

Among the powder flasks are several used by the Texas pioneers. There is a Spanish spur found on the site of the San Saba Mission in Maynard County, and other spurs used by the pioneer Texas cowboys. A gavel made from deer horn, and cartridges used in the British, French and Canadian armies form interesting features of the exhibit.

There is a rare dispatch box from the Napoleonic wars, bearing the personal insignia of Napoleon Bonaparte, an exploding bomb; a set of entrenching instruments which came out shortly after the Civil War, and a Krag Jorgensen bolo bayonet used on a rifle in the Philippines during the Spanish-American War.

Two ancient blunderbusses are shown, one over a hundred years old and used in the British Navy to repel enemies attempting to board a ship, and the other an Oriental blunderbuss with elaborately carved verses from the Koran on the handle.

ARROWHEAD DISPLAY

Photo number five shows a cross-section of the large Arrowhead collection of Dunn's Museum. This collection alone is so imposing that it would take a volume to relate the fascinating history so strangely interweaving love and death and bloody conflict.

Much of this history is peculiar to Texas and Corpus Christi and vicinity. There is for instance an arrowhead that spelled death to an Indian whose skeleton was recently found at Kinney Park, the old homestead where John Dunn was born 85 years ago. Another was taken from the body of an Indian girl killed by the Kiowa Indians in Duval County, in which raid George Swank, later killed in the Mexican raid on Corpus Christi, was wounded. The Duval County raid was the last made by the Indians in this section.

A number of arrowheads were found at the Oso, which was once an Indian Burial Ground. Here, Mr. Dunn found the skeleton of an Indian girl around whose neck was a beautifully graduated mother-of-pearl necklace. A number of arrowheads were picked up at Joe Bluntzer's place near Lipantitlan Lake, and two Comanche spearheads were found at the battleground of Plum Creek near Gonzales.

Marking back to the weird practices of the Indian medicine man is the blow-pipe, which is a stone through which a hole has been drilled. The medicine man when called to attend a patient, first secretes in his mouth a live cricket, then putting his mouth to the large opening and pressing the small opening against the patient's arm, expels the insect. When the blow-pipe is removed, the credulous patient, seeing the insect, believes it to have been expelled from his own body and in many instances miraculously recovers.

The collection also shows several gruesome scalping knives. One was found on the Custer battlefield, one belonged to the Sioux Indians, another pertaining to the Kiowa tribe was dug up near Laredo, and a fourth was found in Bell County.

The Indian Maidens are remembered in the bird-stones worn by brides and the banner stones serving as hair ornaments.

There are also elaborate pendants and curiously wrought necklaces of coral, turquoise and crystal.

Reminiscent of Indian sorcery is a small and curious figure, very heavy, which was attached to the prow of the warrior's canoe to repel evil spirits. Mr. Dunn also has a number of the celebrated "fairy stones" of Virginia, shaped by nature in the form of crosses, and used for good luck charms, curious totem stones representing animals emblematic of the various tribes, and a curious assortment of Indian and Aztec deities and statuettes of the gods of the Cliff Dwellers.

Mr. Dunn has several beautiful obsidian arrowheads, but only one which was found in Texas, being picked up at the Laguna Madre, near Corpus Christi. It

has been presented to the University of Texas. He has an obsidian dagger from the Admiralty Islands, a stone ax from Tasmania and another from New Zealand.

As a relic of pre-historic days, he shows a number of smooth, heavy stones swallowed by the dinasaurus as an aid to digestion.

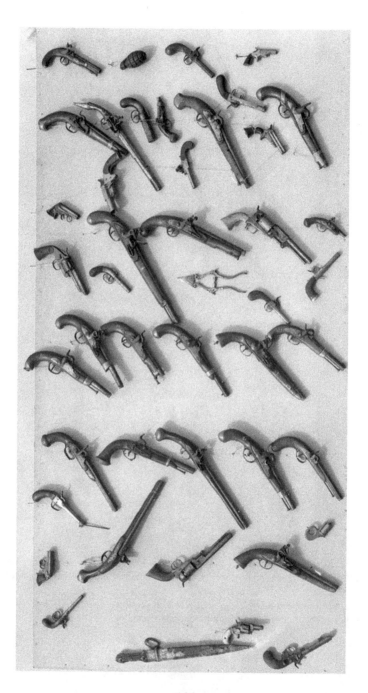

184

PISTOL DISPLAY

Photo number six, showing a few of the pistols from Dunn's Museum, is perhaps one of its largest exhibits, numbering hundreds of weapons nearly every one of which has some noteworthy historical association.

Among outstanding pistols might be mentioned a flintlock pistol used in the Napoleonic Wars, and two said to have been used in the Battle of Waterloo. Occupying a unique position is a Persian pistol with brass stock beautifully engraved. There is a German pistol made at Potsdam during the reign of Frederick the Great, and a pair of Turkish pistols. Several pistols with historical associations peculiar to Texas have been loaned by Mr. Dunn to the Dallas Centennial where they will be shown in the Ex-Ranger's Exhibit. Among the weapons loaned is a pistol belonging to the Mexican Bandit, Hypolita Tapia. This was taken from Tapia on his capture, by Mr. Dunn himself. Another pistol belonged to Cortina the noted border bandit, and was presented to Mr. Dunn by Henry Scott. Also loaned to the Ex-Hangers exhibit, is a pistol belonging to Alberto Garza, alias "Caballo Blanco," who was captured in a running fight with Captain Wallace's Rangers, a pistol used by Martin Woessner, a member of Sibley's brigade, in the battle of Valverde, one belonging to Gus Pool, one of Quantrell's Guerrillas in Missouri, a Colts Dragoon pistol and a Belgian Army pistol.

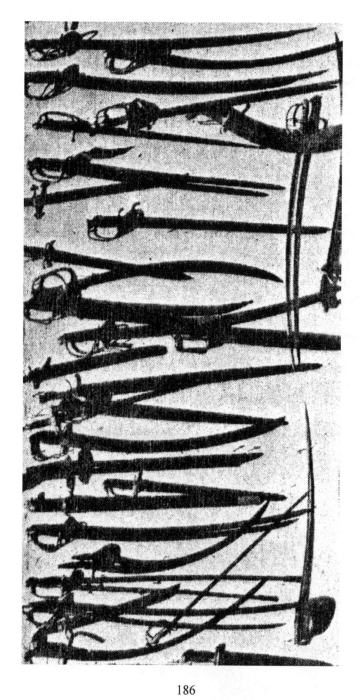

SWORD DISPLAY

Photo number seven shows a few of the historical swords from Dunn's Museum. This particular collection is almost as extensive as the gun and pistol exhibit and possesses an equally historical background. It is composed of weapons ranging from an English sword used in the Revolutionary War to a French Dragoon saber that saw service in the Battle of the Marne.

Among the numerous Confederate swords belonging to the collection the picture shows a cavalry sword from the battle of Antietam, a cutlass used aboard the Merrimac and an artillery sword from the battle of Gettysburg. There are two Union swords, one a cutlass and another a U. S. Naval Sword, surrendered by one of Lt. Kittridge's men captured at Flour Bluff.

Among the foreign swords is one used by Blucher's Dragoons in the battle of Waterloo, a German Uhlan's sword from the World War, a British sword from the Crimean War, a Viking sword from Denmark, and a Turkish scimitar.

There is also a Philippine sword that belonged to one of Aguinaldo's soldiers and a machete from South America. Another ugly machete was the property of a soldier in the ranks of Maceó, the negro general. As a relic of the Mexican War is a U. S. sword that saw service in that conflict, and from the Spanish American War comes a sword used by one of Roosevelt's Rough Riders. Finally, there remains the most gruesome exhibit of all, a Chinese Boxer's executioner's knife.

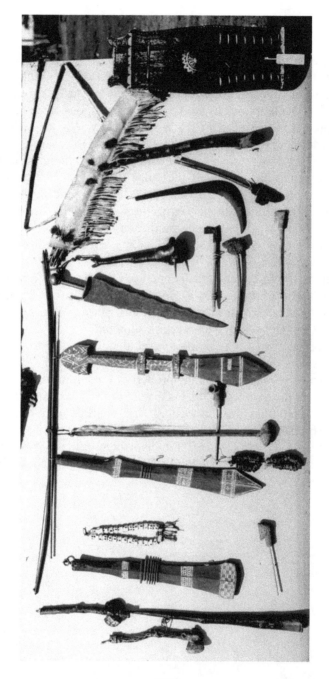

188

CANNIBAL AND PACIFIC ISLAND DISPLAY

Photo number eight shows various weapons from the Cannibal and Pacific Islands. A particularly repulsive war club from the Cannibal Islands is studded with human teeth. Another club comes from the Hawaiian Islands and the boomerang is from Australia. From the African Congo comes a warrior's necklace made from the backbone of a shark and decorated with crocodile teeth.

The headhunter's shield and knife as well as the bow and quiver are from Borneo and there is a pipe from Samoa.

Mr. Dunn's foreign exhibit is quite extensive, containing numerous relics from the tombs of Egypt and from the Aztec temple of Mexico.

His coin collection is of great value containing thousands of rare coins from the time of Caesar and the last days of Pompeii up to modern times.

INDIAN EXHIBIT

Photo number nine shows a part of the Indian Exhibit from Dunn's Museum, Corpus Christi. Perhaps its most important feature, from the standpoint of archeologists, is a four-gallon earthenware pot, found on the shores of the Laguna Madre near Corpus Christi. This pot has been loaned to the University of Texas for its Centennial Exhibit. The only other vessel of its kind found in Texas was discovered by Mr. Jackson, field man for the University.

Also shown in the picture is a "metate", used by Texas Indians to grind corn, and presented to Mr. Dunn by Mr. Townsend of Alpine, Texas, in which locality it was found.

Clumsy flint and obsidian hoes used by Comanche Indians. Flint scrapers for scraping hides, flint scalping knives, curiously shaped ceremonial stones, and a squaw's scalping knife tell strange tales of industry and war. The ornamental buckskin quiver fringed and decorated with feathers, and containing seven arrows, belonged to the Dakota Indians. Among the various peace pipes or "calumets", is one which was the property of Chief Joseph of the Nez Perce Indians. There are bows and arrows and pipes of lava rock belonging to the Modoc tribe, poison mixers with which to poison arrows, granite tomahawks used by the Comanches and Kiowas of Northern Texas, an Apache tom-tom or war drum from Arizona, and a piece of pottery from Lamar County, presented to Mr. Dunn by Mr. Jackson of the University of Texas.

The skull and crossbones shown belonged to a Carancahua Indian and were found on the blind Oso near Corpus Christi and the eight foot rattler whose head rests upon the "metate" was also a native of this city.

APPENDIX FIVE

November 4, 1940

John B. Dunn, Texas Pioneer, Dies Peacefully at 89

Drove Cattle, Worked On River Boat During Colorful Career

Ex-Ranger Had One of Largest Private Museums in U. S.

John B. Dunn who had heard the bullets sing plenty of times in frontier Texas, died peacefully in his bed at a local hospital at 2 o'clock yesterday morning, after a brief illness. He was 89 years of age.

Native Corpus Christian, he played a leading role in the celebrated Old Nuecestown Bandit raid in 1874, and was a member of the Texas Rangers.

For many years he operated Dunn's Museum on Shell Road, which he founded and which contains the largest individually owned private collection in the United States. He started amassing the collection at the age of 17.

Among the survivors are Mrs. Cleveland Wright, of San Antonio, widely-known poet and author whose pen name is Lilith Lorraine, and a grandson Capt. Earl Dunn of the Corpus Christi police force. Others are another grandson, John M. Dunn and four great grandchildren,

Rosary was said last night at 8 o'clock by Father Ralph, who will conduct services at Corpus Christi Cathedral at 9:30 this morning. Burial will be in Rose Hill Cemetery. David T. Peel Funeral Chapel is in charge of the arrangements.

Dunn, also a retired cattleman, was the son of Matthew Dunn, pioneer who came to Corpus Christi with its founder, Capt. H. L. Kinney. Matthew Dunn served as a dispatch bearer under General Zachary Taylor in the Mexican War.

In his younger days, John B. Dunn drove cattle up the trail to Kansas, fired on a Mississippi River steamer, worked in the old packing houses at Rockport, as well as engaging in the cattle business and serving as a Ranger.

He joined that famous force under Capt. Bland Chamberlain when he was 19 and four years later was transferred to the company under the command of Capt. Warren W. Wallace. For his service with the Rangers he received a pension from the government.

In recent years the discovery of oil on his property added materially to his wealth.

He was a member and officer of the Improved Order of Red Men and the Knights and Ladies of Honor. Many have been his contributions to the civic and religious life of Corpus Christi. He was a member of the Catholic Church.

Pallbearers will include Frank Onzon, Tom Whelan, Dick Hatch, Nichols Cantwell, Burton Dunn and Bernard Dunn.

APPENDIX SIX

There were a great many grandchildren of Lawrence Dunn. John B. "Red" Dunn mentions many cousins throughout Perilous Trails of Texas. The chart below shows his many relatives starting with his grandparents, Lawrence Dunn & Ellen O'Riley.

Lawrence Dunn & Ellen O'Riley

    Patrick Dunn & Ellen Wyse
        Edward Dunn
        Katie (Sr. Mary Joseph CSC) Dunn
        Lawrence Dunn
        Mary Dunn & Frank Onzon
        Timothy Dunn
        Eliza Dunn
        Thomas "Kansas City" Dunn
        Annie T. Dunn
        Theresa Dunn

    John Dunn, Sr. & Annie Hyland
        Christopher Dunn
        Nicolas Dunn
        Lawrence Dunn
        Patrick Dunn
        Matthew Dunn
        Joseph Dunn
        Mary Dunn
        Michael Joseph Dunn
        John Patrick Dunn
        Anne Mary Dunn

    Peter Dunn & Margaret Maxwell
        Mary Dunn & James McBride
        Judith Dunn
        Matthew Dunn
        Julia Dunn
        Joseph Dunn
        Theresa Dunn
        Lawrence Dunne
        Lucy Dunn

Matthew Dunn & Sarah Pritchett
John B. "Red" Dunn
Matthew Dunn
James Dunn

Thomas B. Dunn & Catherine Theresa Hickey
Mary Elizabeth Dunn
Lawrence Joseph Dunn
Michel Dunn
Patrick Francis Dunn
Andrew Dunn
Joseph Dunn
Thomas B. Dunn
Catherine Dunn

Lucy Dunn

INDEX

96, 117, 119n, 121, 127, 133, 134, 134n, 137, 140n, 141n, 145, 146, 152, 153, 156, 164, 166, 173, 182, 191

Garza, Alberto (Caballo Blanco), bandit, hide thief, 81, 81n, 85, 185
Givens, Murphy, 2-10
Glen, Sam, ranch foreman, 162
Goliad County, 131
Gonzales, Texas, 4, 17-21, 48, 52, 63, 64, 65, 162
Gray, Mustang, 162
Greene County, Mo., 18
Gregorio, vaquero injured on trail drive, 58, 59
Grulla Motts, 162
Guadalupe River, 19
Guerrero, Coahuila, Mexico, 32, 95, 95n
Gussettville, Texas, 163
Guthrie, Keith, author, 83n, 123n

Hale, Duff, posse member with Henry Scott, 133
Hall, Jesse, captain of Texas Rangers, 118
Hall, John, packery owner, 40
Hallettsville, Texas, 20
Hannigan, Texas Ranger, 52, 53, 57
Hardin, John Wesley, gunslinger, 23, 48n
Harney, Edward, packery manager, 44n
Hart Lake, San Patricio County, 15
Harris, Buck, Texas Ranger, 90, 91
Hatch, George, killed near Reef Road, 6, 96
Hays, Kansas, 6, 57, 58, 59
Hearn's Ferry on the Nueces, 136, 136n
Heath, John, Texas Ranger, 53, 57
Hebert, Rachel Bluntzer, author, 121n
Helm, Jack, State Police captain, 48n
Henry, Julius, with Kinney when he was killed, 162
Hill, The, Hispanic area of Corpus Christi, 9, 133n, 134, 139, 141
Hinojosa, Martin, with Kinney when he was killed, 162
Hodge, James, Dunn's relative, 18
Hodge, Martha Pritchett, Dunn's relative, 18
Holland, Dan, posse member killed, 131
Houston, Texas, 63, 64
Hunter, James M., Corpus Christi livery owner, 105, 105n
Huson, Hobart, author, 131n, 132n, 133n
Hutchinson, steamer, 62

Piedras Negras, Coahuila, Mexico, 95n
Plum Creek, 182
Pollan, Mr. and Mrs. John, yellow fever victims, 27, 28
Pool, Gus (perhaps Poole), Texas Ranger, 5, 47, 49, 50, 51, 52, 53, 57
Portland, Texas, 96n
Poulsin, brought a package from Antwerp, 154, 155
Powell, Billy, freighter in Rockport, 32, 33
Powell family, Rockport, 31
Priour, John M., Texas Ranger and naturalist, 94, 94n
Priour, Theodore, Texas Ranger and rancher, 94, 94n
Pritchett, David, relative, 18
Pritchett, John, relative, 3-4, 17, 18

Quantrill, Charles, 5, 47, 49, 185

Rabb, Dock, Nueces County rancher's son, 151
Rabb, Frank, Nueces County rancher's son, 151
Rabb, Lee, Nueces County rancher's son, 9, 151, 152, 152n
Rabb, Martha, Nueces County rancher, 9, 151
Rachal, Darius C., cattleman, 73, 74
Rains, Louisa, captured in the Nuecestown Raid, 100
Rea, W. L., Refugio County judge, 133n
Red River, 57, 58, 59
Red River County, 18, 53
Reef Road, Corpus Christi, 25, 25n, 96, 96n
Refugio County, 131
Refugio Mission, 131, 132n
Reindeer (ship), 33
Resaca de la Palma, battle, 3, 16, 160
Rhew, Bill, Peñascal posse leader, 75
Richmond, Texas, 64
Ricklefsen, August, Corpus Christi resident, 137, 138
Rincon (North Beach), 16, 40, 41, 161
Rincon de la Boveda, 114n
Rio Grande, 9, 16, 51n, 77n, 91, 93, 94, 95, 118, 132, 132n, 152, 152n, 153, 157
Robelos, Luis, King Ranch vaquero, 111
Roach, storekeeper in Corpus Christi, 134-138
Roark, James Henderson, farmer, 57n
Robb Commission on border violence, 158n
Robinson, Charles M. III, author, 115n, 117n

OTHER BOOKS FROM NUECES PRESS

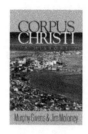  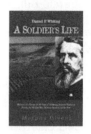

  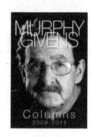

Corpus Christi – A History

1919 The Storm

A Soldier's Life

Great Tales from the History of South Texas

Recollections of Other Days

Columns   2009 – 2011

www.nuecespress.com

Printed in the USA
CPSIA information can be obtained
at www.ICGtesting.com
LVHW041745131223
766027LV00031B/724/J